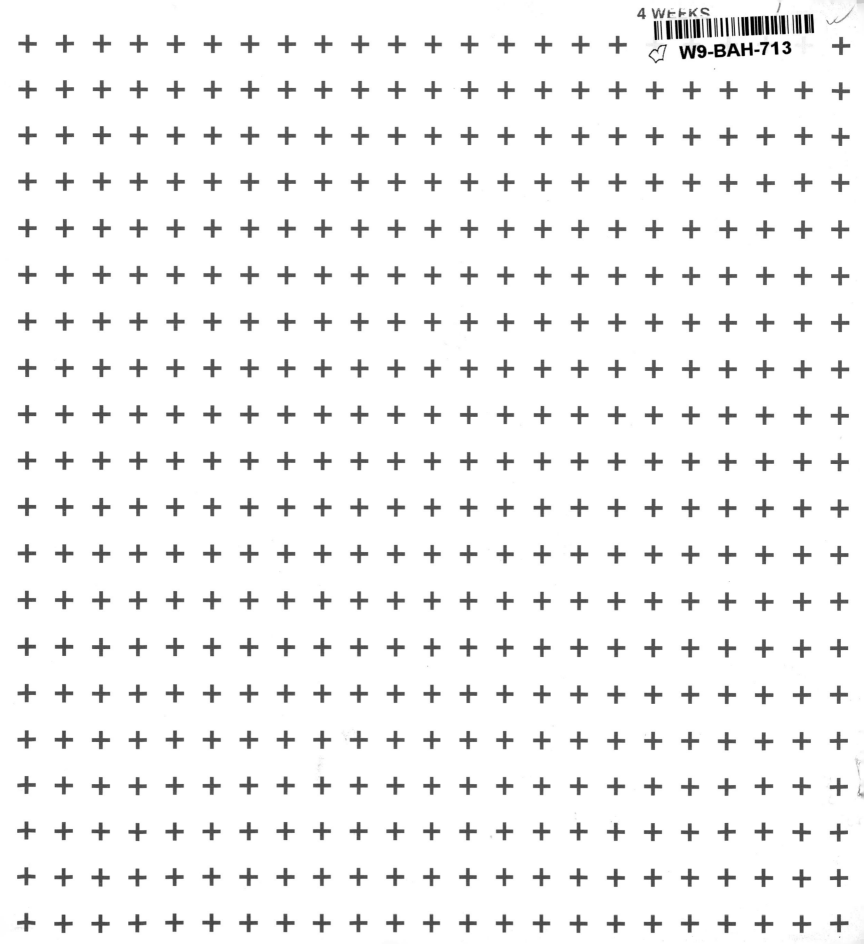

House Plus

House Plus
Imaginative Ideas for Extending Your Home
Phyllis Richardson

With over 300 color illustrations

Thames & Hudson

45.—

Design: Grade Design Consultants

© 2005 Thames & Hudson Ltd, London
Text © 2005 Phyllis Richardson

First published in 2005 in hardcover in the United
States of America by Thames & Hudson Inc.,
500 Fifth Avenue, New York, New York 10110

thamesandhudsonusa.com

Library of Congress Catalog Card Number
2005923451

ISBN-13:   978-0-500-34211-4
ISBN-10:   0-500-34211-3

Printed and bound in China by C S Graphics

People the world over are outgrowing their living space. In London, New York, Sydney and Munich, not to mention the cities in-between, couples, single dwellers and young families are all bursting the boundaries of the Victorian terraced house, the 1920s bungalow, the modern suburban subdivision. The traditional residence, the house, is fast becoming the house plus a bit extra on the side, back, roof even underneath. There are a number of reasons why building on is the preferred option for achieving more space. Prospective extenders may have been put off the idea of a new build by limited available lots, planning restrictions, or the huge financial commitment; while sky-rocketing property prices prohibit the purchase of a larger home in a desirable area. Or they might just like the building they live in, despite its spatial limitations. Whatever their reasons, people are pushing up and out to create a home-office, increase their entertainment or living spaces, or add bedrooms or wings for cross-generational families. A wood-lined roof garden or concrete terrace

Introduction

te

su

bec

or e

addi

Prosp

whole

restricti

rocketin

home in a

they are in

rationale

off

People the world over are outgrowing their living space. In London, New York, Sydney and Munich, not to mention the cities in-between, couples, single dwellers and young families are all bursting the boundaries of the Victorian terraced house, the 1920s bungalow, the modern suburban subdivision. The traditional residence, the house, is fast becoming the house plus a bit extra on the side, back, roof or even underneath. There are a number of reasons why adding on is the preferred option for achieving more space. Prospective extenders may have been put off the idea of a whole new build by limited available lots, planning restrictions, or the huge financial commitment; while sky-rocketing property prices prohibit the purchase of a larger home in a desirable area. Or they might just like the building they are in, despite its spatial limitations. Whatever their rationale, people are pushing up and out to create a home-office, increase their entertainment or living spaces, or add new bedrooms or wings for cross-generational families. A glass pavilion, wood-lined roof garden or concrete terrace

Contents

and pool house that celebrates the contrast between old and new or augments an already pleasing building might just be the solution.

A house addition offers homeowners a way to reconfigure their existing living space, an opportunity to express personal design ideas and creativity or a chance to share in the vision of an architect or designer on a scale less daunting than embarking on the construction of a completely new house. The projects shown on these pages demonstrate that whatever kind of dwelling you start with and for whatever reason you change it, the choice of what to add is as wide and varied as your imagination.

Residential extensions comprise a dazzlingly broad range of styles, forms and materials, from faithful reproductions of an existing structure to marked oppositions. A Californian 1920s Spanish Colonial–style house, for example, might have an addition that mimics the old house right down to the traditional methods used for the stucco. But in the wilds of Scotland, a traditional stone croft might benefit from a fully transparent glass appendage that contrasts starkly with the original building but also sits unintrusively in the landscape. In-between are countless possibilities that vary in degree, ambition and design. An extension can mean adding a simple, but elegant, box with a character of its own, or it can be part of a larger remodel, where the new structure inspires an interior renovation or vice versa. Often when a larger, light-filled space is built on the natural inclination is to take down interior partition walls, allowing light to filter through so that even if the old house remains fairly untouched it is imbued with a new sense of openness and light.

Craving to bring more light indoors is one of the primary reasons people seek to add something contemporary or more up-to-date to their original building. If you live in a nineteenth-century townhouse in New York, London, Amsterdam or Sydney, getting more light into the house might be almost as important as adding a new space itself. Or the idea of having your own version of Mies van der Rohe's Barcelona

Pavilion (1929) glowing gamely in the back garden might be too tempting to pass up. Of course, there are practical issues, such as how to ensure the light-filled box relates to the existing house, how not to deprive yourselves and your neighbours of a sense of privacy, how to get around what are increasingly stringent city building codes. However, in the twenty-first century, when glass technology has evolved to produce materials that are highly energy efficient and structurally sound, the reasons for not using glass, apart from the issue of cost, dwindle. And, as you will see, more than a few residents have been seduced by the glowing possibilities of glass.

The glass box does more than serve as a beacon or bring vast showers of light; it enhances that vital link with the outdoors, which many people feel has been neglected in their living space. The desire for light-filled, open-plan living that connects with the outdoors rather than being closed off from it, is a common drive for extending a living space. Even in parts of the world where the climate is less inviting and where rooms have traditionally been based on a size that is easy to heat, people are embracing the open-plan lifestyle. Its popularity may be attributed to the trend for loft-living or to the resurgence of interest in the glass-walled Modernist houses that introduced luxurious expanses of glazing in domestic spaces in the middle of the twentieth century. Again, with advances in building technology, glazed enclosures can now be kept as warm as fire-lit stone cottages and as structurally sound.

Beyond glass and light construction, materials such as wood, steel, concrete and stone can all be used innovatively, sensitively and appropriately, particularly with older buildings. Decisions about expanding that may begin with a consideration and a real dream of more interior space quickly develop into how that space will be added. While most residents know where they will add, few have a set idea of the style, or even the variety of styles to select from. Choices on everything from wood flooring to acid-etched glass panels, Perspex walls and window frames, ceiling materials to paint colour will affect how the space looks and feels on the inside. But the use of large planes of glass, wood, concrete or stone will obviously have an impact on how the house is viewed from the exterior, by the residents, neighbours and local planning authorities. That is not to say that contrast is impossible to achieve, and in fact a number of the projects shown here demonstrate a huge degree of experimentation. So, anyone who thought extending, rather than starting from scratch, necessarily meant an unacceptable amount of creative compromise should think again. Not everyone will be allowed free reign by their local building authority, but you might be pleasantly surprised at what you can undertake once regulations have been met. And, the materials you choose will ultimately have a huge impact on the feeling you get from the new space.

In the end, extending or adding on to your home is a process of figuring out what your domestic needs really are and then planning how to fulfil them. It can be a very enlightening process, one that not a lot of people might bother with, being more likely to move to a space and fit themselves within it rather than create something unique. This is where it gets exciting. It has to be said that building on also presents great challenges and a degree of risk, but as the houses in these pages amply illustrate, the end result can be something truly wonderful, a vast improvement on the quality of domestic life, whether you are talking about a whole new annexe or simply a glass-enclosed patio space, whether you are wanting to add light or find a retreat, whether you have the urge to blend in or make an unusual architectural statement.

House Plus is organized into five chapters, the first four covering the natural direction of any house's expansion: Above, Behind, Beside, Below. The fifth chapter, Around, encompasses extensions on more than one floor or side of a house, perhaps someone who started with a rear addition and then decided to add a similar structure to the roof. Each of these approaches makes different demands on the style, design and structure of the extension. There is no separate category for frontal extensions, though they do appear, but usually as part of larger makeovers that include more prominent additions elsewhere. It is interesting to note that in many cases front façades are almost sacrosanct, though the occasional raised porch, improved garden or additional skin may enhance the presentation of the entrance or unify an old structure with a new one. None of the projects are solely interior additions, but again, these may happen in the course of other work on houses presented here, such as a free-standing steel framework inserted into a barn that has also been extended beyond the original structure. At the end of the book is a section that focuses on specific materials and methods, giving snapshots of particular details that can distinguish a new extension, enhance a structure or serve as a design theme.

    The aim of the book is to give confidence to homeowners to address the problems of structure, style, harmony and contrast to create a better living space and to show designers and architects the broad range of possibilities they might pursue with a willing client. House extensions are often overlooked architecture projects, but there is something thrilling about rejuvenating and expanding an old, under-used living space into something fresh, modern and welcoming, about meeting the challenge of combining new with old, historic with contemporary and even in considering how our living space can evolve over a lifetime or through generations.

Some of us spend our lives making do with a kitchen that is just a little too small, a living room a little too dark or a house that barely contains the artifacts and motion of our daily lives. This is a book about making our domestic spaces as elastic as our lifestyle, adapting the building to our needs rather than the other way around, and perhaps achieving something creatively satisfying in the process.

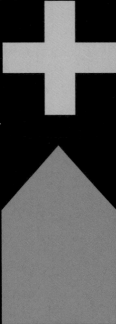

Onwards and upwards, the roof extension seems a logical choice for the vertical urban dweller to continue creating space and to gain free access to a piece of sky and maybe even a bit of greenery. This section features rooftop additions that vary from full rooftop conversions, where whole floors of living space are created from pushing the roofline up and then adding light through larger or unexpected window openings or skylights, to rooftop perches, where a room is added on top and the remainder of the flat roof left open for a terrace, deck space or garden. Then there are roof lanterns, semi-transparent boxes that provide a sheltered entry to the rooftop while also allowing light to pour through the shaft of the stairwell and saturate rooms one, two or even three floors below.

The advantages of a rooftop eyrie may seem blindingly obvious, but sometimes the perception of what lies, tantalizingly, beyond the ceiling only comes once a roofline is punctured and light pours in over hitherto sombre rooms.

The urge to go beyond the roofline and to actually break through the roof space takes a brave character. However worried people are generally about knocking down walls, even when they are assured of structural security, the idea of going up through the roof is a nerve-wracking challenge. It is a journey usually only undertaken if you have made some scouting trips up to the perch on top of your house or apartment building, perhaps via a ladder or fire escape, which in itself has the air of something slightly secretive. Suddenly the unknown territory above is bright with possibilities for entertaining, relaxing, sunbathing or quietly observing the world at treetop level. Breaking through the roof has a distinctly liberating feeling, as if the confines of the physical house have truly been blown open and the chance to form a new perspective and pattern of interior light also unfolds. The combined sense of privacy and freedom offered by rooftop spaces makes them tremendously appealing and costs for a modest rooftop room plus open terrace are comparable to (if the structure is sound) and sometimes less expensive than other types of additions.

Roof Terraces

From sleek modern hardscaped roofs, where concrete and glass are only softened by the sound of a well-placed water feature, to the rooftop jungle, where wood and greenery make the urban environment less urban and more of a retreat, from spaces that teeter over a skyline view to those that are enclosures from the elements with patches of sky carefully framed, the roof terrace is a city dweller's secret place of refuge. Architect Lorcan O'Herlihy's design for a house in Hollywood (see p. 20) is a case study for unexploited rooftop potential. Whereas, before the roof extension, the house 'didn't have a magnificent view', it now boasts a rooftop deck from which it is possible to see not only the city sprawling out below, but also the Pacific Ocean and islands nearly forty miles away. Furthermore, a lavish penthouse bedroom and luxury bathroom with opaque glass and polycarbonate sheeting make even the most private room feel open and light.

Rooms at the Top

Some people are looking to gain more by going up through the roof than a single room and terrace; their aim is to achieve much greater interior space, adding a whole new floor perhaps, while also taking the opportunity to make the floor below much lighter than in the original layout. Planning permission allowing, a new storey answers a lot of problems particularly in densely packed urban sites. In a less than picturesque industrial waterfront neighbourhood in Rotterdam, Mechthild Stuhlmacher and Rien Korteknie have created an extreme version of the rooftop extension in their design for the Parasite house, an entire, mobile dwelling that can be fitted on any flat roof where services can be attached (see p. 34). Their first trial of the Parasite habitation in Rotterdam also provided a rather enviable rooftop terrace space within what is a low-cost housing alternative.

Most of us, however, will have to make do with a single-floor extension, but this too can almost create the feeling of a new habitation, depending on how the flow of light is manipulated. Projects like Sam Marshall's roof extension to a nineteenth-century brick house near Sydney (see p. 28) makes a very modern, compact, but light top-floor suite of rooms with surrounding clerestory windows that bring in plenty of light. An addition to a building in the suburbs of Paris by Jakob + MacFarlane makes use of an array of unusual window openings to brighten a children's playroom (see p. 32). Breaching the roofline at the rear but not the front can help resolve planning issues that stipulate conserving the character of a historic street, while also allowing for much-needed expansion. Other top-floor solutions are more ambitious. For a ground-floor structure in Paris wedged between two much taller buildings, the team at Architecture-Studio created four floors all open to light from above and the exterior windows (see p. 26). Not satisfied merely to fill in the space with an approximation of the surrounding architecture, the architects added volumes that 'bring the sun to the farthest corners of the house'.

Lanterns and Stairs

It is light and more light that is repeated time and again in clients' demands for roof extensions, to the point where some people are not looking for extra space so much as an opening to illuminate the stairwell and surrounding rooms as much as possible. Roof lanterns are more structural than skylights, less imposing than a fully serviced roof addition. In both the roof lantern projects here (see pp 40 and 42), the new, transparent addition also provides permanent access to a newly claimed roof terrace. A stairwell bathed in light proceeds through the light box to the roof itself, which now almost beckons to those below with its warm natural glow.

In most top-floor additions opportunities arise for a creative solution to the age-old problem of dark, awkward or cramped stairwells. The tendency in the projects featured here is for open stairways that allow as much light to flow through as possible via roof lanterns, top-floor windows or even glazing within the rooms. Free-floating stairs make a virtue of the stairwell as an illuminating device and help to create transparency and to minimize any tendency toward darkening rooms with partitions. These projects, which entail both upper- and lower-floor extensions, demonstrate how wedded we are to traditional forms and how innovative we can be.

Nathanson Residence
Hollywood, California
Lorcan O'Herlihy

> A house in Hollywood now boasts a
stunning rooftop eyrie thanks to Lorcan
O'Herlihy architects. The curved shape
of the structure and deck suggests
'a dialogue' with the city and contributes
to the general feeling of openness and
yet seclusion.

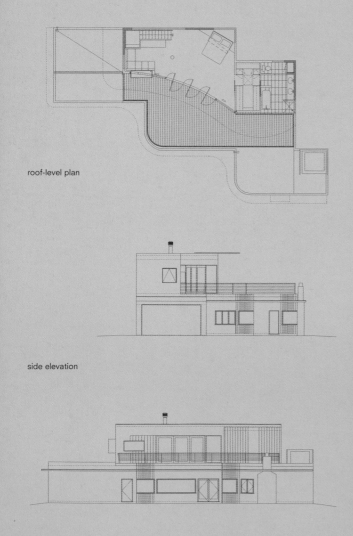

roof-level plan

side elevation

rear elevation

∧ Featuring unexpected practicalities in a grand design, the sitting area has custom-made maple furniture that includes under-seat storage.

A house in the Hollywood hills. The views must be paramount. But in this case they weren't and neither was the attitude to space. The solution: to build up and then look out, to create not just an attic extension but a structure that embraces its privileged position, and enthusiastically at that. The materials: wood decking to emphasize the outdoors and to survive the occasional inclement weather; glass in varying degrees of transparency to let in light but also to provide privacy; and stainless steel in deceptively thin cable for secure but delicate railings. All is executed in a curving form that almost dances in exultation on the roof of the old structure. Lorcan O'Herlihy is known for a particularly vibrant approach to Modernist design, often embracing the clean lines of Modernism but then livening them up with colour and texture. Here, he has given himself, and his clients, over to the thrall of being above it all, not in a

∧ The sweeping curve of the structure creates a landscape of its own on the rooftop. Palm trees, wood decking and a series of large doors make the roof space more inviting.

thickly built urban environment but in the mix of mid-size skyscrapers, hillside vegetation and a view out to the ocean that makes this a perfect little perch for taking it all in.

The extension is more than a stylish sun deck; it also serves a utilitarian purpose. The new structure includes a top-floor bedroom and en suite bathroom with light and transparency in harmony with its windswept peak position. The sitting area, master bedroom and bathroom are all finished with custom-made maple fittings, so the luxury is not only on the outside.

'A house has the potential to engage the city,' says O'Herlihy, and in this goal he has succeeded. The rooftop addition is now a viewing platform, taking advantage of the vistas that the residents knew were there but could not reach. Within the gently sweeping curve, based on the idea of an inverted eye on the city, the bedroom is slightly tucked away from the deck and the bathroom sits on the curve's outside edge, bathing in light; all have views over what lies beyond.

> Rooftop rooms include a bathroom with a glassed-in shower. Panels of frosted and clear glass provide privacy and light.

< Glass panels in the bathroom are repeated on the exterior of the sitting area to balance the materials on the façade. However, here they are backed with wood to provide a greater feeling of intimacy inside.

Rooms at the Top

∧ **Single-level building, Paris**
Designed by Architecture-Studio, this top addition to a ground-floor structure added four floors to fill in a vertical gap between existing buildings. The curved white panels on either side of the exterior follow the line of the traditional buildings on the street, while the wood panels create a more modern façade that allows for an interesting play of light inside the house.

∧ The single-family house is designed around an open central staircase, only bounded by metal grating, so natural light flows between floors. Narrow rectangular window openings add a sense of privacy while still admitting as much sunlight as possible. The spare interior uses such materials as wood and metal to create a changeable backdrop for family furnishings and arrangements.

∧ **Victorian townhouse, near Sydney**
Bold colour highlights the bright interior
of the new space, which includes a
sleeping area, sitting room and bathroom.
The bedroom has clerestory windows
to admit light without affecting privacy.

< On a narrow site, the brick townhouse
was ripe for extension but planning
permission was tricky. Luckily, Sam
Marshall's design for a subtle but modern
rooftop addition won over the planners.

∧ A larger window in the sitting area
amplifies the light in the entire space.
A window seat upholstered in bright red
fabric is a cosy touch and affords a view
over the neighbourhood.

< Urban living, Cologne, Germany
Manuel Herz's 'legal/illegal' extension to a narrow site adheres to building restrictions on the ground floor, which includes the preservation of an entrance gate. The top floor features an 'illegal' design, in sharp contrast with the neighbourhood style, that exceeds restrictions for floor area.

∧ Every surface of the non-orthogonal upper-floor exterior is faceted, allowing for numerous windows and bright interior spaces. Covering the exterior in red polyurethane allowed 'construction without details'. Terraces feature at the rear and side of the building, so that the mass 'steps down' to the ground-floor volume.

∧ Rather than continuing in the same style as the remodelled house, the architects gave the extra floor its own identity, constructing two small 'igloos' for the children, which are clad in zinc. While the shapes and material seem a radical departure, the spaces adhere to regulations regarding the degree of setback and site-specific views.

∧ **Suburban house, Paris**
After remodelling the existing house in 1994, architects Jakob + MacFarlane were asked to return to the project and add another floor, essentially a 40-square-metre (430 square feet) loft space for the children.

ʌ The zinc volumes were broken down
according to the architects' intentions
and tempered by local regulations,
resulting in a series of complex geometric
forms that provide a range of unusual
openings for windows and skylights.

< Balloon framing in pine was prefabricated
and then placed on the roof by crane.
The zinc cladding is robust and malleable,
well-suited to such an irregular form on
an exposed site.

Las Palmas Parasite (LP2)
Rotterdam, the Netherlands
Korteknie Stuhlmacher

∧ Views from the terrace belie Las Palmas's
siting on the rooftop of an abandoned
industrial building.

< The interior of the prefabricated rooftop
house addition is lined with the same
engineered waste wood as was used
to fabricate the exterior structural panels.
However, because of the high degree
of precision involved in pre-cutting the
panels, it gives the impression of a tailor-
made design.

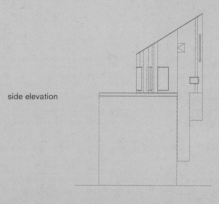

side elevation

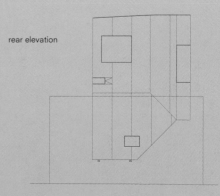

rear elevation

Not an extension or addition in the traditional sense, the Parasite is a semi-independent construction that can be attached to an existing building – ideally a disused warehouse or other light industrial structure or the flat roofs of large buildings – and plugged into the building's services. The result is a dwelling that lives off another building, takes up no new ground space and provides a modern, desirable living environment. Assembled from prefabricated components, the Parasite makes use of fairly low-cost building materials but presents a stylish, unique profile that looks more custom-made than environmentally friendly and offers a promising outlook for many abandoned sites or those considered unsuitable for permanent habitation. The Parasite house grew out of a programme that was created after the appointment of Rotterdam as the Cultural Capital of Europe in 2001 and was inspired by the ideas of temporary and mobile architecture.

It might not create the extension of your dreams but the Parasite could well influence future building. The habitation designed for the roof of the plant room in the Las Palmas building in Rotterdam by architects Mechthild Stuhlmacher and Rien Korteknie is the first of its kind to see completion. The architects found the vast empty roof space an ideal site for their experimental building, which boasts a waterfront view for which many people would pay top prices.

> Walls, floors and roofs of the ecologically sound building were constructed using large, solid, laminated timber panels made from European waste wood and prefabricated off site.

>> The low-cost luxury apartment includes a living space that opens onto a roof terrace overlooking the harbour.

< The bright-green shape of the Parasite house becomes a landmark of high design in a disused waterfront neighbourhood.

< Ripe for parasitic habitation, the disused building becomes home to a penthouse with a luxurious rooftop terrace, amenities more associated with multi-million-pound developments. The house is a self-contained miniature spot of civilization and design awareness amid slabs of grey concrete.

Lanterns and Stairs

∧ **Seattle dwelling, Washington**
In the renovation of a suburban house,
Jim Burton of BLIP Design was pleased
to find that his clients were as interested
in energy conservation as he was. Their
joint commitment to solar energy resulted
in a rooftop lantern that houses the
mechanism for gathering solar power
while also providing a light source that
funnels right through the main stairway
of the house. The roof terrace is now
much more accessible thanks to the
stairway that rises through the lantern.

> The front façade shows the extent of
the exterior and interior renovation with
wood cladding that is carried through
to the design of the rooftop extension.

< Terraced house, London
A very simple rooftop conservatory extension was devised by architect Simon Conder, known for his subtle, elegant approach to expanding structures. Modestly priced, the addition offers a wealth of natural light to the rooms below, a pleasant garden room to enjoy in winter and easy access to the roof space, which is now used as a rooftop garden.

> Inexpensive polycarbonate sheeting and a braced softwood frame made this a highly cost-effective, durable and beautifully transparent space. The polycarbonate also provides more privacy than sheer glass.

Behind

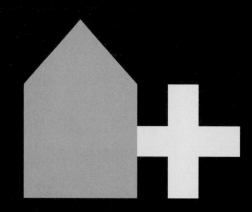

Probably the most common direction to move in when expanding is to the back of a house or apartment on the ground floor. Such a move can take advantage of under-used or unloved portions of a back garden, especially in places where the climate limits the use of the outdoor space to a few months a year. It may mean turning a garden shed into a new dining room or annexing a patio to create a large, open kitchen and dining area that leads directly to the outdoor space, an ideal solution especially for families with young children or for people who like to entertain and are looking for a large, continuous space where people can flow effortlessly between indoors and out. However uninviting the weather may turn, the rear extension is often used to help integrate the outdoors with the living space. Using large windows or sliding glass doors allows more light into the house and the addition of a skylight to the newly projecting space ensures sunlight can penetrate the room at all times of day and in all seasons.

House and Garden

Rear ground-floor extensions present a great opportunity
to engage with the outdoor space. Paul Archer's near
invisible fully glazed extension in London (see p. 56)
amplifies the impact of a small, urban garden by making
a room that is surrounded by and melded with the
plantings and pond outdoors. Also in London, a garden
room designed by the prolific minimalist Simon Conder
has the look and feel of a cosy living space but is fully
glazed on three sides so the greenery of the garden
is ever present in the living space (see p. 52). Not
happy with a mere sliding door to make the transition
to the outdoors seamless, David Adjaye (see p. 58)
created a giant pivoting glass wall and clad the
interior and exterior areas in the same material,
so that house and garden do not meet so much
as transcend boundaries.

Utilitarian Annexes

Not nearly as boring as it sounds, the utilitarian
spaces that can be grafted onto the back of the house
range from a separate apartment for the grandparents
(see p. 62) to the practical and spacious solution
of adding modern bathroom or kitchen facilities.
Utility can have its own beauty, especially when the
creative possibilities of access, light and cladding
are fully explored.

Rooms for Art

Of course, some rear additions are intended to do
more than just add a bit of elbow room. For people
who have grander ambitions for their living space,
the rear extension can be a complete break with the
style and proportions of the existing house. For owners
of a gable-roofed suburban house outside Boston,
Massachusetts, the expansion was an evocation of
a lifestyle change and bore little resemblance to the
original house, focusing on the freedom of working at
home, on the presentation of their large and beloved

collection of contemporary art and on their dedication to fitness and their need to be able to swim and exercise year-round (see p. 66).

Art was also the driving force in an extension on a much more proscribed plot in London (see p. 70). The largely glazed addition creates a great sense of continuity in the somewhat narrow confines of a semi-detached house, allowing the artworks to be spaced throughout and opening the spaces to light.

Not so Basic Box

Even a simple, boxed-in room addition can have a huge impact on the overall living space of the ground floor. Making better use of natural light, modern materials and open-plan design, the effects of the basic box addition go far beyond the added square footage.

From New York to London, projects that are no more than the equivalent of a room at the back help to transform the existing house. The outdoors becomes the focus, rather than an afterthought, and the relatively small, new rooms become a blank canvas for experiments with colour, materials and texture. When Dutch firm One Architecture was devising an extension for a house in the style of a French château, perhaps even they were surprised when the client chose as a starting point something akin to Mies van der Rohe's Farnsworth House (see p. 80). But the large glass window wall brings the fresh greens, browns and blues of trees, lawn, shrubs and swimming pool into view with such immediacy that the landscape, and not the minimal design inside, draws most attention.

Staggering Spaces

Rooms need not be completely made of glass to enhance the outdoor space, though it certainly helps to maintain the focus on the out-of-doors. The way a structure is positioned around the outdoor 'rooms' also helps define the outdoors as a significant part of the living space. Rather than being a straightforward projection at the back of the house, a rear extension can be shaped to highlight areas of the garden for different uses, as a private courtyard and patio area near the house, slightly separate from the main expanse of the rear garden, like the design by Wilkinson King (see p. 88) on the outskirts of London. In the hills outside Los Angeles, architects Marmol Radziner created an extension that expertly mimics the style of the clapboard cottage, but steps up the hillside behind the house and wraps around a treasured oak tree (see p. 92). In Calgary, Canada, where the outdoor space is not really used for nearly ten months of the year, Richard Davignon (see p. 86) extended a modest house that juts out slightly into the rear patio area, a new garden room with lots of light and views to the outdoors, but with the temperate comfort of being safely inside.

The New Conservatories

It is glass that defines the new conservatories, glass boxes that are clean-lined contemporary takes on the old-fashioned conservatory, which has attained a rather fusty image in the last decade. The unfussy, climate-controlled rooms of today take us outside but comfortably weatherproofed.

Pool Views

Pools are no longer a stand-alone luxury. From the mediterranean glamour of the French Riviera (see p. 106) to the rustic elegance of an Irish farmhouse addition (see p. 110), the pool commands its own dedicated structure. Why not? If you are going to have thousands of gallons of pristine water poured into your back garden you should enjoy looking at it as well as swimming in it.

House and Garden

∧ **Single-storey house, Los Angeles**
A reflecting pool casts morning sunlight
onto the masonry walls of this rear
extension by Daly Genik Architects.
The narrow width of the wall and
the corner openings blend indoors
and outdoors.

> The original house was designed by
California Modernist architect Gregory
Ain as part of a residential development
built in the years following World War II.
The new, double-height extension is
wrapped in translucent polycarbonate to
admit light while protecting an extensive
collection of wall-hung textiles.

< The garden was re-designed in consultation with pioneering landscape designer Garrett Eckbo, who had landscaped the original site. Native plants, trees and shrubs create a lush effect, while the resurfaced patio paving reinforces the connection between interior and exterior spaces.

∧ The extended height adds a sense of grandeur to a modest floor space and the maple plywood ceiling softly reflects natural and artificial light. Steel shelving running the full height of the 4.27-metre (14 feet) walls provides storage for books and textiles.

> Nineteenth-century house, London
Architect Simon Conder added a
'crystalline box' to the rear of this house
to produce a garden room. The new
space incorporates an awkward narrow
area that existed between the house and
garage. Materials were cleverly arranged
in this deceptively simple design, which
uses steel beams, great panels of glass
on three sides and dark wood on the
interior and exterior. The roof is a steel
and timber deck finished with concrete
paving slabs to provide a new terrace
for the first floor.

∧ A pebble-lined trench surrounds
the new structure, separating it slightly
from the stone paving and giving it
the appearance of floating. Otherwise
the boundary between indoors and
out is hardly perceptible.

> The architect's goals were transparency
and luminescence. The limestone floor
and white plastered ceiling reflect the
north light that washes through the room.

∧ Terraced house, London

A stunning family and entertaining space has been added to a traditional house by Paul Archer. A far cry from a garden marquee, the glass room has a single solid glass roof, almost unadulterated glass walls, underfloor heating for the winter and wall and floor vents for cooling in summer. An ideal place for dinner parties or reading the Sunday papers when it hasn't quite reached T-shirt weather, the glass room is intended as 'an architecture of invisibility'.

∧ Extending to the sculptural raised beds, shrub and tree planting and the lighted reflecting pool in the garden, the design creates a strong connection between the inward-focused brick structure and the outdoors. Specially designed and coordinating lighting in the garden, pool and extension room displays a variety of colours, which are reflected on the water, adding dimension to the small garden space.

> The room is an inversion of bringing the outdoors in. By placing a transparent, climate-controlled space within a well-planned garden space, a sculptural presence is made of a highly useful room.

v **Townhouse, London**
A continuous flow of space was achieved
by excavating the rear garden of this
nineteenth-century four-storey house.
The basement level, once an awkwardly
accessed, partly submerged space, is now
on a par with the rear garden, which has
been paved in the same material as the
kitchen floor, to extend the interior
beyond the house's end wall.

> Mimicking the glowing glass roof plane
of the extension and opening the entire
end space to the outdoor area, a key
feature of the design by David Adjaye is
the giant pivoting rear window wall. It also
provides extra roof cover in the event of
uninviting London weather. Box planters
and a water feature are part of the
integrated landscaping.

< The galley-style kitchen enhances the uninterrupted flow through the basement floor. Black basalt used on continuous surfaces also draws the space out into the back garden where the elevated terrace, at the far end, is clad in wood to distinguish it from the interiors. Glass panels used along the bathroom wall, left, allow light to glow through to the kitchen area.

**∧ Suburban house,
Kaiserslautern, Germany**
Accommodating different generations of
a family can be difficult, but this addition
by Bayer Uhrig also had to adhere to strict
local building regulations (for example,
no flat roofs). Nonetheless, the result is
a clean-lined, light-filled space.

< Regular wood cladding responds to
the local vernacular but, along with the
overhang of the top floor, stretches
the planning limits to achieve something
more interesting than a carbon copy.

> The new apartment for the residents'
mother is accessed by a separate
entrance; other spaces in the extension
are entered through the existing house.

v **Georgian townhouse, London**
A timber structure was the perfect solution for this extension. Interiors are covered in translucent white Perspex, which gives a bright finish, is moisture resistant and reveals the horizontal window strips that let in natural light.

v 'There is a long tradition of timber extensions to Georgian buildings,' says the architect, Henning Stummel. The timber tower houses two bathrooms and a toilet/utility room, accessed at each floor level. The complete structure could later be removed without compromising the integrity of the existing building.

> As the fenestration would have to be in keeping with the neighbourhood and as none of the rooms are living spaces, Stummel opted to do without windows and to bring in light through the openings, which mirror the plywood strips used for construction. Timber was a very practical choice as all the components had to be carried through the house.

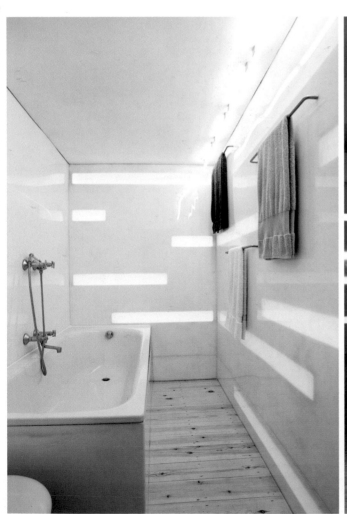

∧ **Rural habitation, near Boston**
A rear extension in Massachusetts uses a high, angled roof and large panes of glass to create a series of light-filled spaces within an open-plan interior. The brief for architects Kennedy & Violich was to provide space for art, exercise, entertaining, work, study and relaxation all within a 306-square-metre (3,300 square feet) addition.

< The real breakthrough for the architects came when they put the swimming pool inside the living area, thus eliminating the need for separate structures. By creating the bridge and mezzanine on top of the pool they made space for an office. Keeping to a palette of wood and concrete enables spaces to flow together. The residents' substantial collection of artworks were also a priority, so the light, while prevalent, is largely indirect and comes through upper windows or from behind walls that house sensitive works on canvas or paper.

<<< From outside, the extension appears as its own complete structure. The light is cleverly angled through the clerestory windows.

<< Continuous spans of wood are used for floor, wall and work surfaces, curving and bending to each new purpose. An office area is sited above the indoor pool.

< The pool water is treated with chemicals that do not give off unpleasant smells. The structure around the pool is used to support the roof and, at the top, to house a variety of mechanical equipment, such as dehumidifiers to protect the artworks.

v Shelves neatly follow the line of the extension, and the architect has used the drop in level to create much-needed space for books and objects in built-in storage.

v The iroko wood cladding on the rear of the extension draws the line of the building to an elegant conclusion while also suggesting a space for cosy retreat in the garden. Iroko wood has a tactile appeal and is very hardy and weather resistant.

> **Semi-detached home, London**
Architect Sanya Polescuk was asked to create a rear addition that would be suitable for use as a private art gallery. The design begins with a glazed space that negotiates the steep slope down from the back of the house to the garden level. Once through this dynamic and transparent transition the structure becomes more solid and enclosed. Artworks that need protection from sunlight are housed in the rear portions of the extension, while a large window wall and glass door make a natural connection to the garden.

∧ **Manhattan apartment**

Aside from more space, an extension to a ground-floor space by Artifact Design + Construction also brought a renewed appreciation of the back garden. This was partly accomplished by the residents' unusual request to move the master bedroom to the front of the house, on the street side, meaning that the main living space sits at the back of the house and opens onto the garden. The steel column supports the rear wall of the four-storey building, and the extended portion stretches beyond it.

∧ Though the siting of the master bedroom on the public side of the house may seem odd, the placement of the living and dining space on the garden has given new dimension to the interior as a whole.

∧ The dropped ceiling panel helps articulate the kitchen space as well as housing lighting and services.

∧ At the new entrance, the master bedroom is separated from the public space by a panel of acid-etched glass. A diagonal wall panel cuts through the ground-floor space from front to back and separates the private spaces (bedroom, study, bathrooms) from the shared areas (entry vestibule, hall, foyer, kitchen, living/dining area).

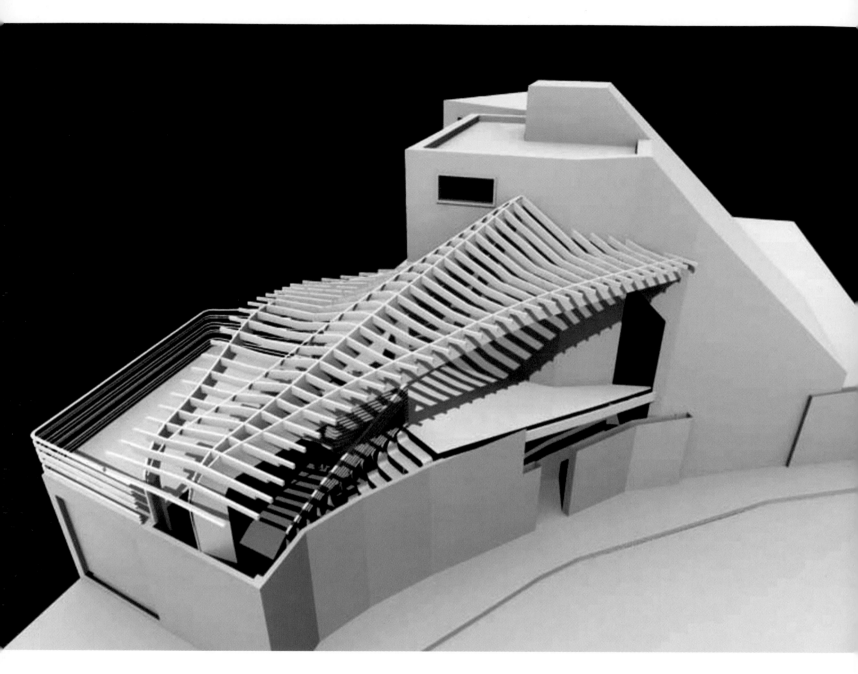

∧ **Late-Modernist house, London**
Some striking innovation by London firm
oceanD was called for in this conversion
and extension of a 1970s house on
a steeply sloping site. The undulating
spinelike structure works as a buttress
and responds to the hillside site. On the
first floor, the extension forms a bridge
that leads to a new mezzanine space,
and both areas are open play spaces
for the children.

∧ The new annexe contains interior
galleries that overlook the existing
three-storey living space. An integrated
carbon-fibre stairway and balustrade
connects the ground level with the sloped
mezzanine. The fluid forms inscribed in
the stair are continued through the walls,
creating varied window openings that
will be enhanced with interactive lighting.

> 1930s house, London

There is a tactile joy in Sanya Polescuk's use of materials in this rear extension to a semi-detached house that complements old brick with new wood. The cedar-clad structure is slightly raised above garden level, by about a metre and a half, to create an interior space that flows easily from the old rooms into the new. The support for the extension, a recessed brick base, is almost invisible; at night, the structure appears to be floating just off the ground.

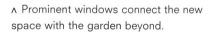

∧ Prominent windows connect the new space with the garden beyond.

> For the new kitchen and family room, the architect used plywood for walls, floors and ceiling to minimize costs and also to create a very robust and unified living area.

∨ **Nineteenth-century house, London**
Wilkinson King's simple room addition on the back of a terraced house forms the garden part of the living space with fully opening rear glass-panel doors. The space gained is not just the new interior but also the garden, which is now effortlessly accessible and present in the overall feel of the interior.

Villa near Eindhoven
the Netherlands
One Architecture

∧ A Modernist-inspired glass pavilion
extension to a villa near Eindhoven
creates the connection to the natural
landscape that the original house was
missing. The contrast with the French
château-style house is intentional, as the
residents wanted something that turned
attention to the garden and woodland.

> A spare interior space is not only
a paean to the designs of Mies van der
Rohe, but a way of letting the colours
and texture of the outdoors permeate
the open living and dining area.

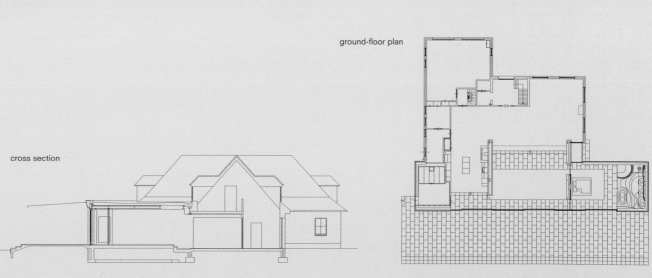

cross section

ground-floor plan

> While the open living space is an essay in white, a more enclosed room has been clad in wood making it cosier and more intimate than the large, public areas. A boxed skylight keeps the room from feeling dark or closeted.

v The smooth granite terrace leads to the lawn and swimming pool (not shown). The stainless-steel cornice above the windows contains a five-metre (16 feet) movable awning, heating and anti-bug systems and lighting fixtures.

French château meets Miesian pavilion. Tastes change, it is safe to say, even in the style of the house you want to live in. For someone whose love of France inspired him to build a house in the style of a French château in the early 1980s, the leap to the peerless Modernism of Mies van der Rohe some fifteen years later may have surprised him as much as it did his architects. But, there was never any doubt that the result would be something worth talking about. Having purchased most of the large woodland around his house in the Netherlands, the client felt that the inward-looking villa was no longer in tune with the family's lifestyle. He asked Dutch team One Architecture to create a structure that emphasized the relationship between indoors and outdoors. The architects presented their client with a few villa examples to choose from and of those it was Mies van der Rohe's Farnsworth House that captured his attention. It seems an unlikely coupling, but the decision to welcome the open living style of a Modernist design helped bridge the gap between the medieval romantic style of the main house and the desire for a more contemporary design that embraced the natural setting.

Now, the red-tiled hipped roof rising above an elegant horizontal form in granite, steel and glass seems perhaps unusual but also logical in the progression from interior-based design to the more outward-looking style of the glass box. The open plan of the extension serves as a sheltered transition from the château to the garden and swimming pool, leading the eye out of the wide window wall to the greenery beyond. A wide terrace continues the lines of the new addition but also marks the last step toward the garden and the first approach into the house from outside. The terrace also provides a generous space for outdoor entertaining and family gatherings, which was an important part of the design brief.

With the garden and swimming pool clearly visible through the continuous glass wall, that sense of involving the outdoor environment with the interior living space is achieved. The Modernist palette, which uses minimal colour and decoration, turns attention to the outdoors. White and black are offset by the greens and blues outside. At night, when the colour cannot be borrowed from the garden, striking red and blue curtain panels are drawn, making a vivid splash of colour and ensuring that the space is never cold or clinical. Materials have been employed thoughtfully and methodically, the grey-green granite having both a natural affinity with the landscape and with the cool textural quality of Modernism.

∧ Large expanses of glass create an
aura of glamour and luxury. At night, the
lighting in the exposed interior makes a
dramatic impact.

∧ Alternatively, boldly coloured curtain panels ensure privacy while also adding colour to the neutral interior.

Stucco bungalow, Calgary, Canada
Architect Richard Davignon added a
cool modern garden room to the back
of a modest home to make use of
outdoor space that was only comfortably
usable for about three months of the year.
Adding a spacious kitchen with oversized
vertical windows overlooking the patio
garden as well as a generously sized
living area increased the overall use
of the interior space. The extension
also brings in much more natural light
to counter those dark days of winter.
The new room steps slightly into the
garden area, making a more interesting
outdoor space.

> **London townhouse**

Transparency is everywhere in this cubic extension. Inside the ample new spaces created by architects Wilkinson King, the eye is always taking in a bit of sky and greenery, whether through the vast panes of the glass walls, the ceiling or the more enclosed skylight. In a place where light is at a premium and the outdoor spaces are not usable year-round, the generous use of glazing amplifies the effect of the garden.

<< Large, fully opening doors emphasize the relationship between outdoor and interior rooms, making an easy connection and flow between spaces.

< Stepping the rooms around small areas of landscaping creates more interest in the garden despite taking up the outdoor space. An inviting, protected and private-seeming courtyard space has been created, making an ideal outdoor room for more specialized planting or outdoor sculpture.

< Clapboard cottage, near Los Angeles
In the verdant hills above LA, a 102-square-
metre (1100 square feet) 1923 cottage
was refurbished and 307 square metres
(3300 square feet) added by architects
Marmol Radziner. Known for their
conservation and preservation work,
the architects made the extension's
exterior virtually indistinguishable from
the original building by maintaining
the green-painted clapboard skin.

∧ Interior spaces were modernized and
opened up while the rustic cottage details,
such as the open beams, chunky fireplace
and chimney breast, were kept.

∧ According to the architects, 'the new master bedroom suite is perched like a treehouse' on the hillside that has been incorporated into the design of the house. It is accessed by a steel-clad bridge from the main living areas.

> Forming a new interior courtyard, the design also links the house to the hillside setting. The architects went to great lengths to preserve the central oak tree, the details of the existing clapboard style and the shingled pitched roof, which blend nicely with the mature vegetation of the site.

Tall Acres
Pittsford, New York
Studio For Architecture

> An addition contrasts in form and
material to the original 1970s suburban
home but achieves a balance of internal
volumes and creates a sheltered porch.

cross section

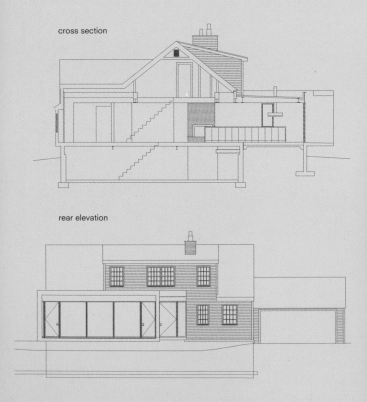

rear elevation

<< A polished black concrete shell encloses a glass-and-metal box, a modern, light-filled addition to the existing saltbox-style structure. Poured concrete slabs on the floor, walls and ceiling create a porch, while openings allow air and light to circulate.

< Set on two parallel concrete foundations, the basic form is framed in timber.

< The construction photo shows how the new structure flows into the ground floor of the existing house.

< The interior of the new addition is open-plan with partitions rather than solid walls separating different areas. The use of glass on three sides also contributes to the light, open character of the interior.

< As the addition meets the existing structure, the ceiling slopes upward, following the roofline of the 1970s house. Windows inserted into the existing roof gables keep the light flowing through the interiors of the old and new spaces.

This is a project of visual contradictions. It appears as if great liberties have been taken. A sweet, white New England saltbox has been lumbered with a dark, solid mass. However, on closer inspection the transparency of the solid form becomes more apparent as does the real vintage of the 'saltbox'. Rather than desecrating a period clapboard house, the architect actually started out with a 1970s, vinyl-sided suburban version. The contrast of style, form and materials became the theme for the addition. There would be no effort to mimic the original form except perhaps in scale and a general simplicity of design and right angles. Ironically, it is the polished black concrete form, flowing into the old house, that opens up the whole plan with its ample glazing. Its mass was meant by the architect as a counterweight to the existing house and at 75 tons it surely does that, but it also provokes an interesting debate about the value of old versus new, organic versus man-made.

The concrete addition rests on two existing parallel foundation walls and cantilevers into and out of the house, counterbalancing the weight, colour, structure and the general 'impermanence of the house', according to Studio For Architecture. The architects playfully oppose the weightiness of the addition by setting it on top of the concrete bars, so it appears to hover off the ground next to the seemingly lightweight original house. The living spaces under the old hip-roofed house are modernized with sculptural wall planes and the use of skylights. There is no denying the greater sense of openness and light that the large, unobstructed windows bring to the extension and to the old structure. The architects made sure that a light, sculptural theme carried through. Opening up ceilings to follow the structural A-frame of the old house inside and then inserting glazing within the gable brings more natural light in without touching the roofline. This way, the interior of both the new and existing portions of the house are unified; once inside, there is not a jarring sense of moving between old and new but a continuous flow of light, airy living space. Back outside, a wide, rectangular porch was created using the concrete base, walls and roof with open gaps at the sides and top, which, like most details in the scheme, ensure the all-important circulation of light and air.

> **Victorian terraced house, London**

What began as a simple rear extension became a series of innovative glazed additions. On the ground floor, an added room has a glass end wall but is further enhanced by a semi-transparent roof that is also a glowing terrace space. From the upper-ground floor, a doorway leads to this highly unusual terrace with a flight of stairs to the garden. At left, M³ Architects of London made the extension double height to let even more light into the interior stairwell.

The client also decided to add to the roof of the house, so the architects devised a volume set within the parapet wall that does not go beyond the roofline of neighbouring houses. The full width and height of the structure is glazed to admit natural light to the new top-floor space.

>> A dazzling terrace floor, the tempered glass is also the roof of the ground-floor extension.

∧ The kitchen leads to the new living-area addition.

< An interplay of transparent surfaces and light, the ground-floor extension is a peaceful area in which to relax.

∧ Conservation area home, London
A wasted outdoor storage space was covered with a glass canopy to expand the kitchen and relate the whole house to the garden in a design for a young family by M³ Architects. Light enters the kitchen through large clerestory windows and filters deeper into the other interior rooms.

> Set in a conservation area, the house is subject to strict planning regulations, so the scale of the extension had to be in keeping with the proportions of the house. Yet, at night, the degree of transparency makes the addition seem much larger than it is.

∧ Making maximum use of awkward garden space, the architects spanned the area between the garden wall and the house with a glass canopy that expands the kitchen/dining area and brings vast amounts of light into the rest of the ground floor.

< The glass structure makes a subtle intervention on the exterior of the house, sitting well within the perimeter, but creating more space than is obvious from the outside.

∧ Even the existing rooms farther inside benefit from the light box addition at the rear.

> 1930s villa, French Riviera

As if being on the French Riviera were not luxurious enough, this cool, Modernist-style glass extension creates a truly exquisite hideaway or entertainment venue at the back of the existing villa. The low-lying concrete structure by Rudy Ricciotti is faced entirely in glass and looks out onto a pool running parallel and just as seamlessly. The pool's outer edge perches precariously at the cliff edge. No perceptible boundaries interrupt the surfaces from the floor of the living area to the terrace to the pool's liquid blue.

>> White concrete blends with the stone and vegetation, while the overhanging roof gives shade and a feeling of retreat. As it is set on a steep hillside, the open glass living room and terrace are actually very private areas.

∧ Oaks, cypresses and other trees and
shrubs also make the pavilion and pool
a private retreat despite being so open.
The roof of the addition was landscaped
to occupy an almost cave-like position
in the hillside, a discreetly glamorous
composition.

> Stunning views of the Mediterranean
Sea can be had from the house, terrace
and pool. Water from the pool falls freely
over its edge into a basin on the steep
hillside below. The residents have placed
nets below to catch anything else that
might go over.

< Farm building, County Cork, Ireland
In a climate where outdoor swimming
is only possible (with any level of comfort)
during a few months of the year, enclosure
is a necessity. Hardly ever, though, is it
achieved with such grace and beauty
as in this addition. Architects Springett
Mackay designed not just a shelter for
swimming but a structure that feels
slightly ethereal with light entering
through various arched openings and
reflecting hazily off the water's surface.
The pool house is actually located in the
old stable block, which was gutted and
re-roofed before the pool was inserted.
The wall openings are part of the original
form of the stables.

∧ Alongside the pool enclosure, a glass-lined gallery space paved in Irish blue limestone provides a sheltered circulation area beyond the sanctuary of the pool.

∧ Through the gallery you can see the original stone used for the stable block.

Harris Pool House
Palm Springs, California
Marmol Radziner

> Almost wholly transparent, the pool house has walls that open fully to allow a view through the interior, across the pool and toward the original, Richard Neutra–designed house, which was also restored by the architects.

∧ The house is seemingly without walls. The great, expansive openings are mirrored by the wide roof overhangs and paving, creating a feeling of freedom and luxury.

> The low horizontal design is highly suitable for the desert landscape, where natural vegetation is low-growing and shade trees are rare.

In 1998, the architectural practice Marmol Radziner was called in to renovate a classic work of California Modernism: the 1946 Kaufmann House designed by the pioneer of American Modernism, Richard Neutra. In the course of the restoration, the architects were asked to add a pool house that would accommodate guests and would contain some of the equipment for family entertainment not in the main house. A state-of-the-art audiovisual system, a gym with steam room and a full kitchen were incorporated. Perhaps Neutra's biggest contribution to architecture was his emphasis on the relationship between indoors and out, and the architects, while not trying to replicate the details of the original house, made sure the addition was as open to the natural setting as possible. As the house is in the Southern California desert, this did not pose any real problems, but the degree of openness achieved is quite remarkable.

The walls are fully opening, so the desert breeze floats freely through the interior. But, it isn't only the warm breeze or the cool night air that flows through the house; as the architects explain, 'one virtually sees through the structure', across the pool and the native plantings to the newly renovated Modernist masterpiece. The glass doors and open plan of the pool house encourage easy circulation between indoors and out, and also provide a new vantage point from which to enjoy the original building.

By no means a reconstruction of a Richard Neutra design, the wide open feeling, the low, horizontal plan and the large, sheltering roof overhangs of the pool house are all elements that have sprung from the Modernist sketchbook. They are also appropriate to the hot climate, where shade and unobstructed ventilation are key to comfort. The fact that these elements also produce a structure of cool elegance may explain the renewed appreciation for Modernist-inspired design.

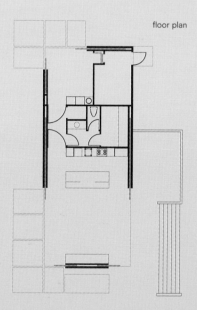

floor plan

< Paving surrounds the pool, but native plants have been used as much as possible to create a particularly lush oasis in the desert.

v The pool house seems to stand alone but has a very conscious visual relationship with the main house, making the pool area feel much more inhabited and part of the entire house design.

< French-style house, Kortrijk, Belgium
A pool house can be much more than
a storeroom or a place to hang towels.
In this extension, architect Vincent Van
Duysen produced a free-standing garden
pavilion that includes space for cooking
and eating, ideal for outdoor entertaining.

v Using crisp geometries and devoid of
ornament, the pool house is a markedly
modern departure from the house,
an 'exciting confrontation', according
to the architect. The anthracite-coloured
wall separates the main house, garden
and pool from adjacent outbuildings.

Beside

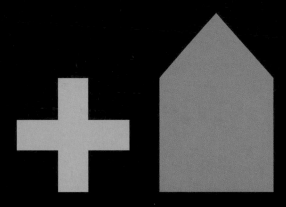

A side extension is not always inherently different from something added to the rear of a house except that building out sideways can entail more reconstruction as the natural openings that lead to a garden or patio may not exist and the house may have to be opened up substantially to accommodate grafting onto the side. In some cases a side extension is chosen to amplify the whole house, extending two or more spaces, rather than just adding a room. Here, side additions are used for such reasons as filling in unused space between the existing house and another structure, like a garage or outbuilding, or creating a logical extension from the house to the property line. Garden rooms, common to rear extensions as seen in the previous chapter, are sometimes more easily added to the side, especially in a rural or suburban setting where lots are not so restricted. Thereby, the rear façade of the existing house, which might be of historic interest or value, can be preserved. Lengthwise side extensions can also link spaces through such additions as a sun porch or glazed corridor.

Sidelights

It seems like an act of covering over to open up, but the horizontal extension that brings in more light is not as illogical as it might sound, as materials and light sources play a vital role. Featuring continuous skylights and glass panels to bring added shelter and light, a new sun porch and circulation area is grafted onto the entire length of a traditional wood house in Japan (see p. 124). Worlds away in Austria, a family farmhouse, built around a central courtyard, that accommodates three generations of the family was given a facelift by architect Hans Gangoly (see p. 126). An expansive glazed living area now links formerly separate rooms and offers a much more transparency and modern open living.

In-Between

In the process of renovating old agrarian buildings, adding a room or rooms between existing structures can be a very good way of achieving highly desirable open-plan living space that is not often found in rural domestic dwellings. Though linking separate structures of the same period with a new structure made of modern materials can be a tricky business, architects Labics have done just that in the countryside north of Rome. For a couple with a large extended family wanting to create an expansive retreat, they successfully renovated a farmhouse that was built as part of a marshland reclamation project in the 1930s. At the same time, they slipped in an elegant glass insertion that creates space for the family to share with weekend guests while preserving private areas within the older structures on either side (see p. 136). Norwegian architects Jarmund Vigsnæs (JVA) worked a similar magic with an old mud and stone stable building on Mallorca, adding rooms between and beside and highlighting the whole linear structure with a long, rectangular swimming pool set in a luxuriously wide terrace (see p. 130). The materials used were more consistent with the original structure, so the long, low series of room appears as a seamless whole.

In a suburban setting, German architecture firm Neugebauer + Rösch created a bright, modern new living space next to a traditional-style 1920s house that had little character worth emulating (see p. 142). The programme consisted of renovating the main house and then adding a distinctly modern and modular-looking side extension that made a logical progression from the carport to the house interior and eliminated an awkward unsheltered transition from outside to in. The new structure, though contrasting in style, is sympathetic in proportion and overall makes a refreshing addition to the standard suburban dwelling.

Up and Down

It is an ambitious project that adds more than one floor to a building, no matter where its position. But adding something onto the side that projects beyond the first floor and is therefore highly visible from the street, obviously throws up questions of style and planning restrictions. These projects are all on the adventurous side, departing markedly from the buildings they extend and showing unabashed pride in their innovation. The modular wooden block form used by Archifactory to add a whole new apartment to a suburban German residence (see p. 146), the Cubist-inspired two-storey addition to an Australian house by Stephen Varady (see p. 148) and the modular planes of an exterior renovation by Drewes + Strenge (see p. 150) all explore and push new forms and materials. In these projects, the aim was certainly not to blend in, rather to differentiate, and yet somehow maintain a sense of balance and harmony with the original house.

Winter Gardens

Glass and stone, opposing forces or mutual friends? Glazed volumes added to the rustic hardiness of rural buildings bring a touch of modernity without compromising the traditional style of the older structures. The use of glass can also be less intrusive, allowing the existing house to remain visible and present in the new design. The addition of a glazed roof to the top of a garden wall next to an old stone cottage creates something radically new but also historically familiar. Who hasn't visited an eighteenth- or nineteenth-century orangery or winter garden built to keep non-native plant species in harsher climates? The tradition, in England, at least, where two of our projects are located, is well-established, even if the current form is more linear, less ornate and somehow more daring. Whether positioned on the back or the side, the glass patio addition makes an ideal venue for garden parties or family use during inclement weather but also on fine days when the blue sky becomes part of the interior charm. Paul Archer's glazed roof structure (see p. 156), which presents a seamless transparent ceiling, was built for the director of a glass company who is involved in developing the latest technology in structural glazing. Filling the space between a seventeenth-century cottage and a more modern block wall it really does represent the marriage of antique and modern building practice. Similarly, the glass addition to a nineteenth-century brick cottage by Deborah Saunt and David Hills, enhances the character of both materials and creates that highly sought-after link between darkened period interior and the outdoors (see p. 164). By contrast, German architects and8, use glass to create a transition from the old structure to the new, but chose the comforting properties of wood to enclose a side extension (see p. 160). The winter garden link brings ample natural light, while the wood cladding signals the warmth and welcome of shelter.

Sidelights

∧ **Moth House, Nagano Prefecture, Japan**
An elongated porch structure was attached
to the side of an existing house located in a
wooded area of central Japan. Architectural
practice Atelier Bow-Wow stressed
lightness and transparency in the project.

∧ The dark wood of the existing structure
contrasts with the white-painted wood
of the addition. The transparent roof,
open slatted wood construction and
series of sliding doors allow the gentle,
dappled sunlight to filter through.

<< Farmhouse, Burgenland, Austria
A small, nineteenth-century farmhouse has been given a modern update with a glass living room and entrance extension by Hans Gangoly.

< Glass walls and the long narrow skylight illuminate the new living room and make the transition between the inside and outside areas 'soft', according to the architect, 'without strong contrasts'.

∧ Running along one of the house's four wings, the glass extension helps to accommodate three generations of the same family. The grandparents occupy the rooms at the opposite side of the house to the rest of the family.

∧ The new, enclosed entrance offers protection from the elements while entering the house but still allows free vistas through the large glass walls and ceiling.

> With its traditional tile oven at the centre, the original farmhouse kitchen is seamlessly united with the new glass living room.

In-Between

> **Farm outbuildings, Mallorca**
A luxurious holiday home was made from
an old ox shed and other outbuildings
by adding a private swimming pool
and rooms on either side of the existing
buildings. Stone and wood are in keeping
with the style of the old buildings and
neighbouring houses.

∧ Despite its rustic origins, the house's interior has been finished to a very high standard.

< Norwegian architects Jarmund Vigsnæs transformed the decaying old buildings into an exquisite retreat by using a simple arrangement of shapes and materials.

v The generous wide limestone terrace lends itself to entertaining on warm summer nights.

> New rooms were cut into the natural, terraced hillside and have views over the valley of central Mallorca.

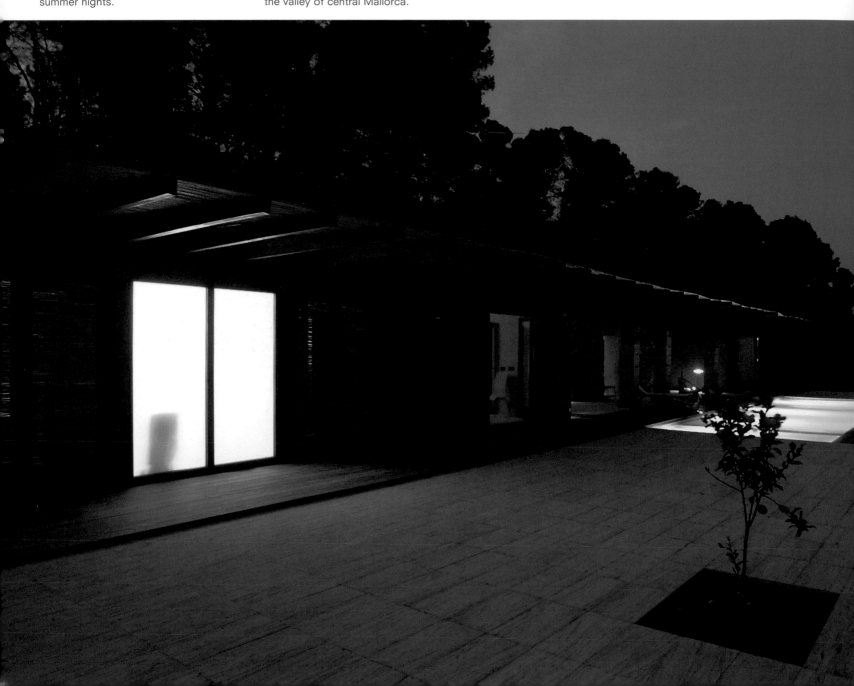

Podere 43
North of Rome, Italy
Labics

> A modern living and dining area was added in a large extension to a 1930s farmhouse north of Rome. The stone wall at right is part of the original stone barn. The clients, who use the house on weekends and holidays, were primarily concerned with comfort, hence the very generous living spaces.

< Off the living room, an area is made into a winter garden with a glass wall and ceiling and indoor pergola to filter the sunlight. Wood flooring alternates with polished concrete.

front elevation

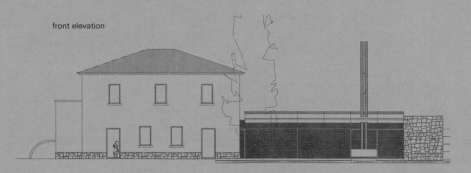

cross section

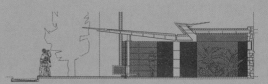

ʌ The old barn is now the greater part of the new, open living space on the ground floor that flows into the old house. At right, a former shed is now guest quarters complete with kitchenette.

The original farmhouse was built as part of a marshland reclamation project in the 1930s. It has now been transformed into a modern retreat for a couple with a young family for whom having a place in which to gather the extended family is of great importance. The residents also wanted a high level of comfort so all modern amenities were included. The Roman architecture firm of Labics renovated the old house while preserving its general interior character but then added ample living space and guest quarters by building off the old barn and sheds. The long low stone wall of the barn hides a glazed addition that connects to the main house, while a sheltered porch now leads to the new guest wing. Not only is the general living space larger and more accessible, it is also distinctly separate from the bedrooms, which are located on the first floor of the main house.

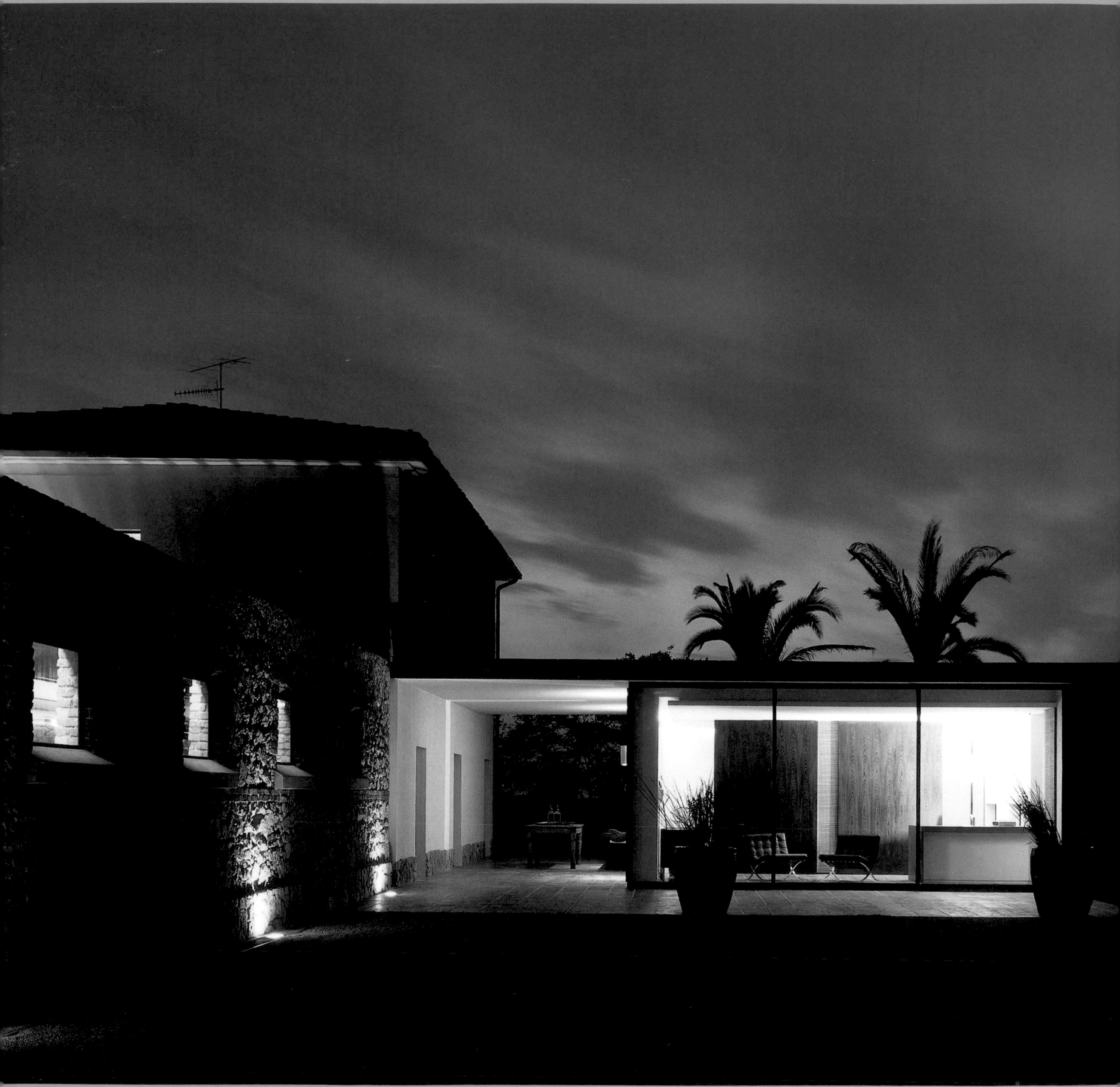

The guest quarters have their own living room and mini kitchen but are not cut off inhospitably from the main living areas. The ground floor is almost all one large space for gathering and circulation, with glass doors leading to what the architects term the 'outdoor living space', an immaculate deck space with a tranquil water basin in one corner. The house is surrounded by well-kept lawns and patios to encourage the use of the outdoor spaces.

A house that was once one of a number of identical, old-fashioned dwellings built by the Italian government, now has a singular, open and modern character, suitable for a contemporary lifestyle but also rooted in the ideal of family unity.

< Stylish, self-contained guest quarters
are private but still connected to the main
living space.

v The living room fireplace extrudes
beyond the glass wall to the exterior
where wood decking and a corner water
basin create a relaxing, comfortable
outdoor room.

∧ 1920s house, near Stuttgart, Germany
Architects Neugebauer + Rösch renovated
and enlarged this suburban house to
accommodate a modern family of four.
Exterior details of the original house,
like the front entrance with its 'dancing'
concrete steps, were also smartened
up in the process.

∧ Disused space between the carport
and the house was filled in to form a new
kitchen and dining room on the ground
floor. The house sits on a sharply sloping
site, so a lower-ground floor was also
created at the rear.

< Wood cladding distinguishes the
addition, as does a metal skin wall
that rises up to become a parapet next
to the original gable roof. While a narrow
window at the front ensures privacy, glass
doors at the back make the dining room
a bright, light-filled space.

∧ From the rear, the full extent of the addition can be seen. A living area, kitchen and dining area were added to the ground floor, while the lower-ground floor provides more living space. The first floor contains three bedrooms and storage space. Large glass doors and windows take full advantage of natural light.

> The architects' renovation included highly refined detailing, such as this polished wood and chrome spiral staircase that is open at the sides so as not to impede the flow of light between floors.

Up and Down

∧ 1940s house, Dortmund, Germany
An enclosed terrace is one of the
unexpected features of a side extension
to a suburban house conceived by
Archifactory. The wooden construction
lends itself to an inviting outdoor
environment.

<< Inspired by the work of American
sculptor Donald Judd, the architects
used solid wood planks to create a single
'compact and heavy' form. Hence the
lack of eaves, roof drains, chimney and
canopy. The windows, too, are flush with
the walls, in keeping with the smooth
planes. The extension envelops the
garage on ground level.

< The wood's texture and warm uneven
colour softens the monolithic form of
the building and helps to tone down the
overall contrast with the pitched roof and
rendered structures on either side. The
large glass door at the rear, together with
the landscaping, brings the outdoors in.

> **City dwelling, Sydney**
Facing the common problem of stairs
and light, architect Stephen Varady
carved irregular window openings
wherever possible on this two-floor
extension to a house. This large landing
window ensures that the stairs are
drenched with natural light.

v The exterior form of the stairway
was inspired by Marcel Duchamp's
<u>Nude Descending a Staircase No. 2</u>,
with the descent marked by a Cubist
assemblage of forms. However, the side
position and vegetation means that the
construction is not overwhelming in
the neighbourhood context.

< The design included the alteration of the entry courtyard, a kitchen extension, a new bar area and an all-glass bath, all of which the architect viewed as 'a dynamic intersection of sculptural elements'. The sculptural quality is carried through to the exterior form, which mimics some of the cut-outs and angles used to achieve the interior spaces of the existing house.

Multi-Generational House
Westphalia, Germany
Drewes + Strenge

carport and roof-
terrace elevation

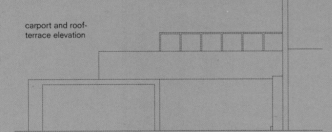

side elevation

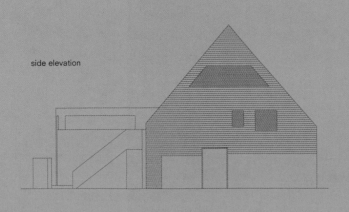

∧ Concrete, steel and glass panels
distinguish a new terrace designed
for a young family sharing a house
with grandparents in Germany.

> By altering only one façade and creating
outdoor spaces in a fresh, modern style,
the architects gave the younger residents
a house incorporating their identity while
preserving the traditional elements on
the interior and on the other sides of
the house.

< Concrete was used to create the
new carport. Clever positioning of the
new elements mean they cannot be
overlooked by neighbours.

'A typical generation conflict,' is how Frank Drewes of the firm Drewes + Strenge describes
the problem that inspired the garden addition to this 1950s suburban house in Westphalia,
Germany. A married couple with three young children share a house with the wife's parents
and would like to claim a portion of the residence as their own without disturbing the comfort
and familiarity of the parents' home. The older generation maintain their household on the
ground floor, while their daughter and her family live upstairs. For the moment at least, the
house needs to accommodate two distinct lifestyles.

Rather than focusing on the decided internal arrangement of spaces, which would
not be altered out of respect to the grandparents, the architects wholly redesigned one
façade and a series of garden areas, including a carport and new entrance, to provide what
is essentially a separate approach and private entrance for the young family. The other sides
of the house and the gardens retain their traditional character but are not really visible from
the new entry. While the vernacular pitched roof and brick façade have been preserved
on those areas untouched by the new build, the addition pointedly uses uncompromisingly
modern materials. Bare concrete, natural wood, Cor-ten steel, asphalt and gravel are arranged
in a series of connected planes to form the separate terrace and entry areas and to gently
screen the altered façade from the traditional entrance. As a crowning touch, the new front
door is painted apple green to signal a fresh, youthful environment.

Only constituting one quarter of the overall exterior space, the new area still gives
the younger inhabitants a real sense of their own identity within the family home. Small but
significant gestures help to heighten this feeling, like the garden on top of the new, concrete
carport that offers a private outdoor space for the couple to entertain or sit alone. Although
this project is not an extension in the sense of expanding the internal area of the house,
it is certainly an important expansion for this family scenario, a way of addressing the need
for personal taste within an older tradition while making everybody happy. Drewes and
Strenge have fortunately managed to bridge the generation gap, or at least dress it well.

<< A series of discreet concrete planes acts as screens, so that the traditional entrance and gardens are not visible from the new entrance.

< Neatly stacked wood is another intelligent screening device to enclose the new private entrance and outdoor area.

<< The vine-covered area is the more traditional side of the house. The glass panels provide privacy on the terrace that sits above the new carport.

Winter Gardens

> **Seventeenth-century cottage, Bristol, UK**
Within the bounds of an unremarkable wall, Paul Archer placed a glass roof, virtually invisible from a distance but covering a modern-rustic conservatory space. The glass roof slides into the existing stonework with minimal intrusion on the character of the old house.

∧ Robust and yet unobtrusive, the glass
roof provides a sheltered outdoor space
to which the owners can retreat in bad
weather and can view skies better in
fairer times.

∧ The exterior of the cottage has retained
its traditional stone cladding and gables.
Even its 1960s block wall is nearly intact,
though now restored more sympathetically
with matching stone.

> The floor tiles continue from the secluded patio to the rest of the garden, a unifying element that leads the eye and guests toward the outdoor area. A water feature is created from the textured laying of the bricks at right.

∧ **Detached house, near Berlin**
Nominated for a German Timber
Construction Prize in 2002, this extension
to a house was nicknamed the 'kids'
house' by the architects, and8, as it
provides two children's bedrooms and
a play area. Attached to the ground floor
of the twentieth-century house, the new
building contrasts with the traditional
style in its bold use of larch strips and
wood decking.

< Wood and wavy shapes make a cosy
and playful structure that happily recalls a
garden playhouse but is at the same time
a sophisticated approach to the limited
space and other building restrictions. The
appealing wood building is connected to
the main house by a glass 'winter garden',
which is used by the children as a play
area in the cold months.

<< The shape of the winter garden's roof and the curve of the playhouse join in the rhythm of the main house's shape while using contrasting materials. The winter garden's roof is more closely aligned with the style of the main house and makes a gentle transition to the kids' house, which is more of a private retreat.

< Reached by ladder, the winter garden's loft becomes a playspace in the winter. The use of wood throughout makes the rooms feel warm and intimate despite the chilly view outside.

< With the charm of a traditional winter garden, the interior of the new orangery has a high-tech glass design that ensures greater transparency than was available in the past – no metal supports – along with up-to-date climate control.

v Solidity and transparency coexist in the brick and glass addition. Structural glass set within the old brick perimeter walls offers protection as well as free access to natural light.

< Brick cottage, Norfolk, UK
The nineteenth-century cottage near the east coast of England retains its traditional character while a low-key side extension possesses hidden drama.

< Designed by London architects
Deborah Saunt and David Hills, the
illuminated orangery is an atmospheric
all-weather dining space.

∧ Through the garden wall. A surprisingly
modern and magical space sits behind
the humble old façade.

When the words basement extension or conversion are uttered thoughts often turn to a well-insulated rumpus room for the children, a darkened hideaway for a billiard table or, if you are thinking slightly more rustic but more up-market, a wine cellar. None of the following projects fit these categories. Underground here means both under and out. The extension may shift earth below ground, but then sweep outward into the garden, creating space beyond the original footprint of the house or simply encouraging the flow through the interior toward the outside.

In some cases a steep hillside site prompts the architect to consider digging that much-needed space out of the ground. In urban areas where tall, narrow buildings have been constructed with the ground level at the rear of the house lower than at the front, many half-submerged rooms already in use are turned to the obvious advantage of increasing space and light.

From Basement to Garden Room

In places where the rear garden sits above the floor level of the house, there are a number of ways in which a partly subterranean extension helps bring the outdoor space more firmly into the overall plan of the house. The garden can be excavated farther to create more outdoor space that is level with the basement room, and a surprising amount of natural light can be drawn in with the generous use of skylights or even glazed roofing. In London, where basement rooms are as much an integral part of the Victorian house structure as any of the upper floors, the problem of how to open up these dark spaces is well known. Though the rooms might be positioned only slightly below ground at the rear of the building, they might previously have been connected with the back garden via a narrow stone flight of steps leading up to ground level and so have poor access to the garden space. The room is not totally submerged but the barrier of the ground level often makes it feel that way. Architects Paul Archer (see p. 172) and Springett Mackay (see p. 174) employ some fairly simple methods to great impact to enable slightly sunken indoor spaces to flow easily into the garden. First, they turned the original rooms from poky compartments to wide, open rooms with broader access to and from the main building. Second, they excavated an area of the garden directly beyond the extension to create a level transition to the outdoors so that the garden has an immediate contact with the house. Finally, they used large windows, skylights and generous sliding doors to help these new rooms feed into the garden, thus amplifying the interior space even further and bringing in a great deal more light.

Carved from the Hillside

People whose houses are situated on steep, hillside plots often take advantage of a great view but neglect the rear garden altogether due to the daunting prospect of excavation and underpinning; for example, a deck sitting up on stilts might be the extent of their hillside occupation. Depending on the site, the process of excavating and infilling to create a level surface may be no more problematic than most new construction. And, the potential for new space, whether as an enclosed interior or a more usable outdoor area, is enormous. In Brisbane, Australia, the possibility for using the partly excavated area below a house was exploited by the residents and m³architecture (see p. 176). They used the undercroft along the back of a standard bungalow to create rooms for grown children, which will become office space for the parents once the children finally flee the nest. The brief to address the stages of family life also resulted in wings that extend beyond the rear of the house to redefine the garden area and ultimately to make better and more interesting use of the outdoor space.

A sloping hillside was also the inspiration for a light-flooded addition and re-landscaped garden design in California by architects Daly Genik (see p. 180). The judicious use of concrete as seismic stabilizing material and construction component helped create a bright new open living and dining space that flows easily into a level garden. In the following chapter Australian architects Donovan Hill have produced a remarkable example of what a rear garden excavation can achieve (see p. 236).

Going Underground

Of course not all basement extensions will provide great opportunities to engage with the outdoors or bring in huge quantities of natural light. Sometimes, digging down is simply the best way to add space, whether due to structural concerns, planning restrictions for exterior structures or costs. But there is still plenty of room for creativity and innovation. As with a roof addition, an extension below the existing house level will present great potential in the design of the stairs. A subterranean extension in Southern California (see p. 186) uses the opportunity of the stair insertion to create a sculptural block that juts through the interior and provides storage and display space while also guiding the flow into the lower rooms. These subterranean spaces vary in height as the architect, though restricted by the height of the existing building, was able to achieve much greater ceiling height in certain parts of the basement.

The issue of lighting will always be a key aspect of interior spaces, particularly in basement rooms and the answer is not always the most obvious one. As architect David Adjaye has shown in his extension for an artist in London (see p. 190), there are a number of ways to bring light in and it is usually a combination of methods that works to the best effect. His lower-ground-floor extension is covered over in glass block, so that while an elegant patio extends beyond the new dining area on the first floor, the painting studio on the floor below receives light through the ceiling and through a courtyard light well that was left open at the far end of the space.

One of the most stunning examples of a basement addition that is flooded with natural light is the extension by GAD Architecture to a traditional-style farmhouse on the outskirts of Istanbul, Turkey (see p. 192). A luxurious layout of end-to-end swimming pools extends from indoors to out with the basement portion lit by inspired roof cut-outs that appear as elliptical holes in the garden lawn. Like Alice going down the rabbit hole, or as in an enchanted garden, the design has a fantasy quality that goes beyond practical or even grand expectations to deliver space that is a visual and physical delight.

All these projects argue the positive qualities of the basement space, that it is no longer the poor cousin to the rooms higher up. Instead of a dark, closed-in room, a subterranean extension becomes a house's hidden jewel.

From Basement to Garden Room

> Terraced house, London

A rear extension and renovation of the lower-ground floor of a nineteenth-century house by Paul Archer brings light inside and easy access outside. A large 'scallop' was dug from the back garden and turf added at basement level. When the glass doors slide into wall recesses the new lawn feels like part of the dining area.

v The new kitchen is streamlined and infused with light from the addition. The worktops were cast on site from white sand, white marble chippings and sand.

<< One sheet of double-glazing, the extension's roof allows light to pour through the new space into the existing rooms, emphasizing the circulation with the outdoors.

< The form of the extension was twisted slightly to preserve an existing tree. The silver steps at right link the old back door to the new outdoor space and are another wide means of access (no struggling with children through narrow doorways) to the elevated lawn.

< The original garden sat one metre above lower-ground level. A new retaining wall had to be added, but this was extended to produce the extra space for a patio and courtyard on the same level as the kitchen. The architects explain that the extension is 'half bunker, half hide, due to the sense of enclosure and protection one feels inside and its low profile'. Steel and wood elements also mitigate against overexposure.

<< **Townhouse, London**
Architects Springett Mackay created a bright kitchen and garden room by excavating and redeeming a half-submerged basement space.

< Making a virtue of the lower-ground-floor position, the architects designed a skylight, windows and oversized sliding glass doors to let in vast amounts of light. Privacy is not compromised as the extension is at such a low level.

∧ **Bungalow, near Brisbane, Australia**
In a suburb, Michael Banney and Ben Vielle of m³architecture were asked to augment a hip-roofed bungalow that sits on a steep hillside. The aim was to integrate the house more fully with the natural setting while providing rooms for the clients' grown children that could easily be transformed for other uses once the children have left home.

< Two bedrooms, or studies, and a bathroom were added. This bedroom (or home office) opens directly to the hillside. The work space is truly indoor-outdoor, with the desk surface and flooring extending beyond the enclosed interior.

∧ Along the back of the house, the bathroom is part of a series of rooms formed by partly excavating the 'undercroft'. The view from the bathroom looks to the new upper-floor deck.

> Glass, concrete, pine, plywood flooring and black-painted plywood partitions comprise a functional palette that allows the rooms to be adapted for different uses. Simple materials focus attention on the landscape's colour and texture.

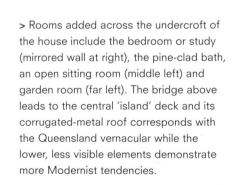

> Rooms added across the undercroft of the house include the bedroom or study (mirrored wall at right), the pine-clad bath, an open sitting room (middle left) and garden room (far left). The bridge above leads to the central 'island' deck and its corrugated-metal roof corresponds with the Queensland vernacular while the lower, less visible elements demonstrate more Modernist tendencies.

< The sloping underside of the house has been highlighted by the architects with their 'hyperbolic wall' covered in polycarbonate sheeting and backlit in red. This gesture of colour and material stands out from the subdued character of the extension's main elements.

Beverley House
Venice, California
Daly Genik

< By levelling out a hillside site below a 1920s bungalow in Venice, California, architects Daly Genik created a series of light, open spaces. A roof deck above the new extension is surrounded by a specially developed metal mesh to offer a degree of privacy while allowing light to filter through. Another similar terrace was added on top of the garage, which sits at the other end of the garden.

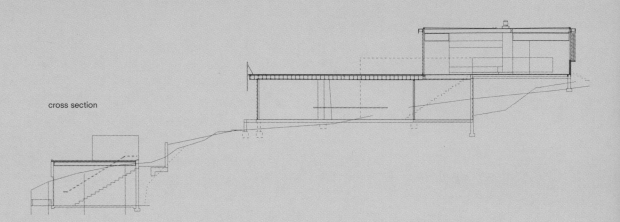

cross section

> Most of the bungalow's skin was left intact and the original entrance to the house was preserved. The wood cladding is new, as is the clerestory window, visible at right.

> The interior of the original house has been opened up and light brought in through the windows and minimal use of partitions. The bookcases and fire surround adhere to the Craftsman tradition of high-quality built-in furnishings.

On a sloping 'street-to-street' site, a 1920s bungalow drew the attention of a professional couple with a teenage son. The typically dark, enclosed interior, however, was not as appealing as the outdoor space and setting. The low-slung, dimly lit bungalow style that grew from the Craftsman tradition in California belies the area's temperate climate, creating more protection from the sun than being open to it. The architects immediately saw that the house needed to be 'turned inside out', that the conventional spaces inside the bungalow should be brought out into the open by moving them down to garden level, and that the remaining space at street level should be opened up. To bring in more light to the upper floor, the roof was lifted and clerestory windows inserted. Unnecessary walls were also eliminated from the plan and partitions that do not reach full ceiling height define spaces, allowing light to pass freely through the formerly darkened areas.

Downstairs, in the space created by excavating the hillside, a light-filled kitchen and dining area was designed. A fully glazed corner enclosure sits on a triangular concrete slab that projects beyond the interior space like a ship's prow into the newly claimed rear garden. These lower-floor rooms are anything but cavernous, as light pours in from the opened space upstairs and the glass side walls.

In an area of pronounced seismic activity, such excavation might seem a major challenge, but the architects found the prospect unintimidating, saying that the soil on site is very stable and the concrete elements, though they have a seismic role, serve to further the form and theme of the design. The act of excavating meant working with the landscape and integrating the house more with the outdoors, something that is of prime importance where the climate is so benign and people spend a large part of the year living happily on the threshold between indoors and out.

∧ Enthusiastic cooks, the couple now
have on the lower-ground floor a large,
open-plan kitchen and dining area,
as well as an additional bedroom and
a study at rear.

> The architects are committed to
dissolving barriers between the indoor
and outdoor environment. Emphasizing
that blend are the concrete base that
projects well beyond the door, the fully
glazed corner entry and the close planting
around the new structure.

Going Underground

> Post-and-beam house, Southern California

A 110-square-metre (1200 square foot) excavation beneath an existing house set on a steep hillside resulted in a sculptural array of rooms designed by Patrick Tighe. The extension leads from the living quarters above to the garden below, negotiating the drop in elevation.

>> Ceiling heights, dictated by the existing building, vary and the rooms are partly defined by tilting wall planes, which add dynamism and light to the underground spaces. However, the architect tried to expand as much as possible: the highest point is in the music room, which rises to almost five metres, an unusually grand gesture for a dugout room.

<< Adjacent to the staircase, the bathroom is walled by sheets of opaque, laminated glass and the shower cubicle projects over the kitchenette. The bathroom includes a horizontal plane of stainless steel that anchors the lavatory and penetrates the glass wall.

< Cut away at the intersection of the bathroom, the angled stair wall reveals the contrasting materials and allows light to reach the bathing space. When the lights inside the bathroom are on they give a glowing cornice detail. Cutaways in other walls expose shifting perspectives and a variety of focal points within the new rooms.

> The entertainment space overlooks the lower-ground floor and entry to the garden. The sculptural stair wall rises to become a soffit that contains the mechanical and sound systems, a 'floating form' that gives height and shape to the whole programme of rooms.

<<< **Huguenot house, London**
In an old silkweaver's house owned by artist Chris Ofili, architect David Adjaye completely redesigned the interior spaces, extended the first floor and converted the ground-floor garden storeroom into a generous studio. The new ground-floor façade with its sliding and folding glass panels gives an idea of the modern transformation within.

<< At the rear of the house, the first-floor interior has been extended and enclosed in glass to create a new dining area, while the roof of the former storeroom has been paved with glass brick to let light into the new studio below. The result is a series of glowing rooms.

< Light comes from three sources: the glass-block ceiling; the addition of a small open court at the end of the space, which is screened in glass and allows light reflected from the wall to penetrate the studio; and carefully coordinated artificial elements.

< The exterior pool is matched by another body of water indoors. Plans show how the architects carved out space from the hillside below the house while maintaining a traditional-style structure above ground. This house, like many such projects is about wrestling with contradictions. Looking at the house from the road, you would be hard pressed to guess how modern its design is; just as, while having a leisurely swim beneath the garden and looking out at the water dropping over the hillside you would find that the confined spaces of a nineteenth-century dwelling seem much farther away than a few floors.

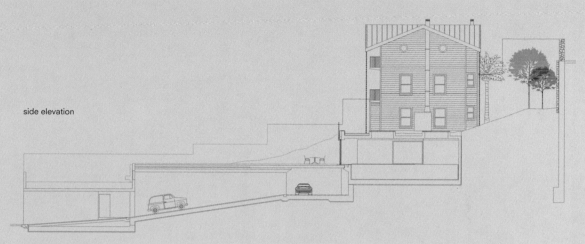

side elevation

v A dining area was created in the underground extension, which also houses the private swimming pool.

v The chalet-style, gable-roofed house adheres to local planning type, but modern elements start to emerge in the rear glazing and the neat stone paving leading out toward the pool area.

The house itself is original only in that it is a nearly exact copy of a house built on the site in the nineteenth century. Strict planning laws in this area of Istanbul precluded a modern house but did not prohibit a dramatic and almost hidden underground extension, not at all obvious from the approach to the residence. With the house sitting prettily on a hillside overlooking the Bosphorus, the architects went to work carving out three more floors of modern living areas from the steep hillside below, doubling the overall space. A lower level holds a swimming pool and gym, a kitchen and dining room and a bamboo garden spreading out toward the sea. Close inspection of the ovoid holes in the grass reveal that they are actually skylights into another pool area below and the experience is like stumbling across a secret world beneath your feet. The idea of the basement pool also has a historic reference since many of the old houses here were once built with holding areas underneath for boats. But again, the effect is much more than historic allusion. The architects were inspired by the idea of bringing water into the house and carried it through in dramatic fashion by creating indoor and outdoor swimming pools that are aligned to 'appear connected when viewed from outside, as if water were rushing through the glass door from one pool to the other'. Equally dramatic is the view from inside, 'where water appears to flood the outdoor pool and disappear over the edge of the garden into the Bosphorus'. In actual fact, the two pools are separated by a narrow path. Such visual sleights of hand are both subtle and expansive, like the overall insertion that adheres to planning requirements while greatly amplifying the space.

∧ Wood cladding and decking create a comfortable outdoor sitting and dining area that also respects local vernacular style. The wood will weather noticeably and beautifully in the sea air. Retaining 'the traditional topography of the chalet house', as required, the architects managed also to create a new, distinctive and luxurious living environment.

∧ A series of areas step down from the back of the house toward the sea. The water appears to fall off the edge of the garden, a visual trick that extends the presence of the garden almost to the sea. In reality, the water is caught in a trough and re-circulated to the pool. Stone paving provides ample room for lounging.

> Sculptural pond-like cut-outs in the lawn set below the level of the outdoor pool are actually skylights that illuminate the indoor pool area underground. These fanciful elements, the architects say, are 'reminiscent of the cut-outs Gordon Matta-Clark rendered into buildings in the 1970s'.

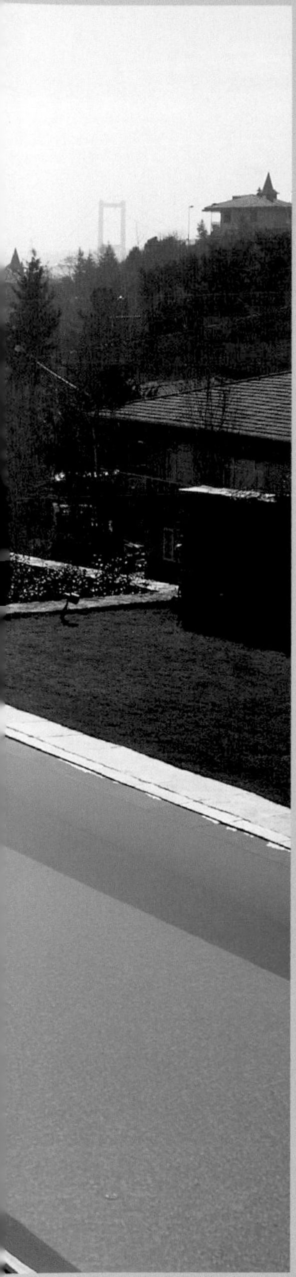

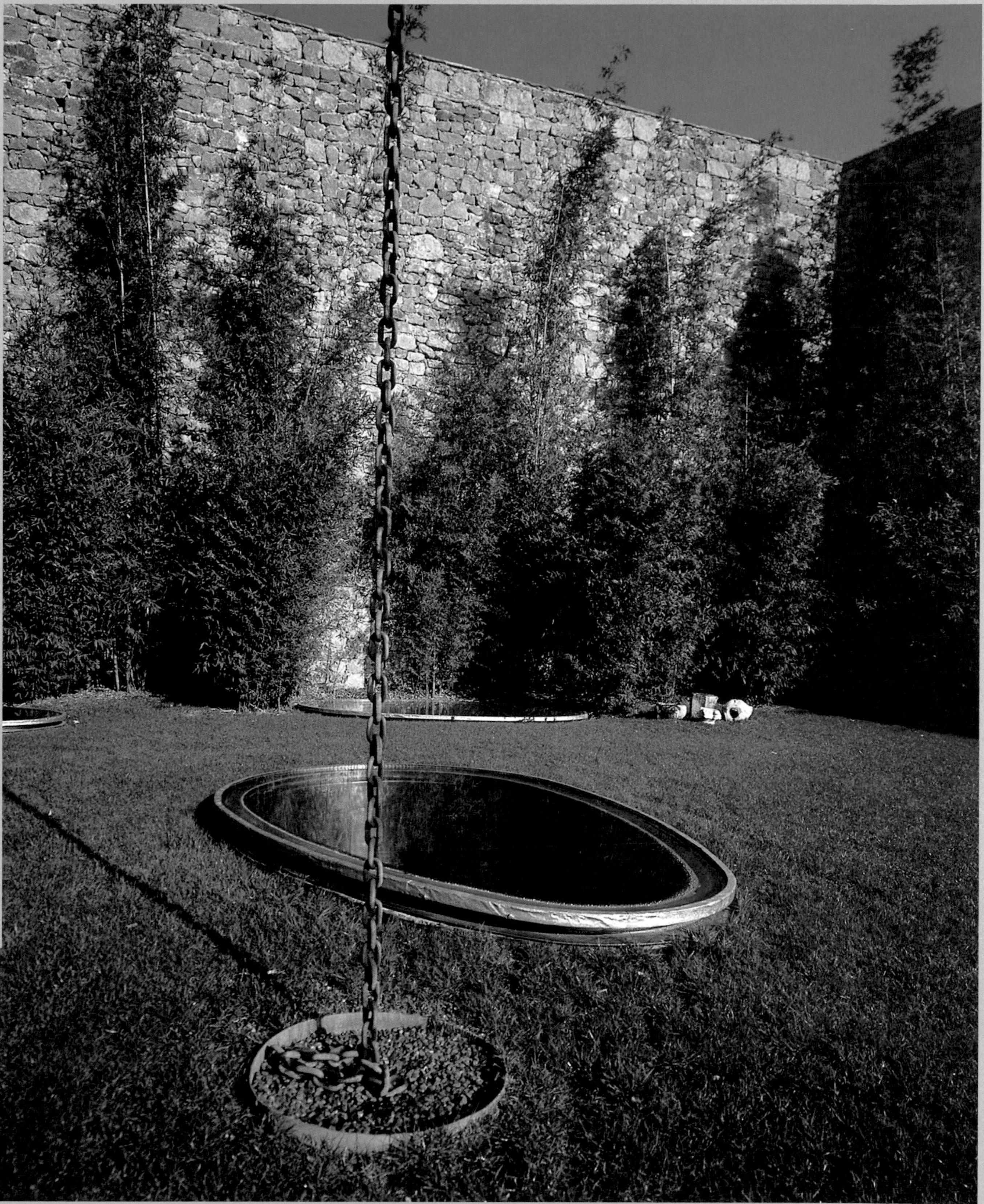

> **Log house, Yamanashi Prefecture, Japan**
A basement addition is given a light, delicate character with an open, slatted wood porch by Atelier Bow-Wow. The overall effect is simple yet striking in the interplay of light and materials.

∧ The concrete wall enclosing the new basement space is counterbalanced by the wood elements that emphasize the horizontal perspective.

> A roof terrace sits on top of the porch, adding two levels of outdoor space to the house. The whole structure is in harmony with the existing log house while at the same time appearing more modern in its rectilinear form.

Around

Extending a house is not always simply a question of adding a room to the roof, garden, side or basement. Even a two-storey addition may not augment your living space to a satisfying degree. It is not that you need a new house, it may well be that once you have decided on a style and form for a glass-walled garden room, you come to the conclusion that a matching lightbox on the roof would complete the picture. Or perhaps the house suffers from such an overall lack of free-flowing space that it requires interventions at different points to open up a view on one side while pulling out a wall on another. It may just be that the whole series of rooms needs rethinking, re-organizing and refurbishing, the result of which is a programme of new construction that still leaves the original house intact but surrounds it in a bold new skin or a defining arrangement of new shapes. Some of the most remarkable house extensions open up more than one floor or plane, reworking a disused industrial building or wrapping up a common suburban bungalow in a ribbon of new rooms to bring space, light and comfort to all aspects of the structure.

Reconfiguring

Changing the arrangement of the interior spaces is
often part of the programme when an extension is built.
A rear bedroom easily transforms into a living room or
kitchen and dining area when the back of the house
is expanded and the garden made more accessible.
A roof extension that brings more light, might influence
the arrangement of upstairs bedrooms or indeed enable
movement of all the private rooms upstairs while
keeping the ground floor for public spaces. Moving
within the house is a familiar practice, especially for
those who occupy period properties where rooms have
long since lost their original functions as things like
indoor plumbing and central heating have come along.
But modern houses often need re-arranging, even those
that were built to order in the first place. A Chicago
house (see p. 206), for example, was built by architects
Valerio Dewalt Train in 1989, but they were asked
back ten years later to add on. A 'tin can' volume now
intersects with the upper floors and helps open the
transitional area between bedrooms and workrooms
while also providing a grand view of the city.

In contrast, Douglas Garofalo's digitally
inspired extensions for two houses in the American
midwest are spectacularly modern gestures for older
dwellings. One (see p. 210) wraps a ribbon of green
fibreglass around a boxy house to produce extruding
glazed pods for living and a vertiginous observation
deck for birdwatching. The other (see p. 216) exploits
the flexibility of titanium cladding to envelop a series
of farm buildings, making one continuous complex
of living spaces for a large extended family. Another
example using farm buildings is a holiday retreat
in Maryland, USA, re-fitted and stabilized by W
Architecture (see p. 214). Inserting a glass box that
projects out and below the main structure allowed
the old barn exterior to stand in its rough-aged glory
while adding space for guests and the display of
a substantial art collection inside glazed sections.

Material juxtapositions may sound like a recipe for disharmony, but looking at the projects shown here the contrast of materials – hard glass with equally hard stone or wood – suggests a continuity of sorts, of materials with structural integrity and natural appeal.

Reconfiguring the layout of the house is often a case of exploding the box, adding a room, a roof terrace, a rear terrace, a new façade and even new cladding. Norwegian architects Jarmund Vigsnæs converted an old industrial forge into a spacious, open-plan house by 'hanging boxes' within the great interior volume and pushing out to create a first-floor balcony and up to make use of the wide flat roof (see p. 222). Within the lofty interior an open staircase leaves all the interventions visible and readable as constructed spaces. Concentrating much more on the outward possibilities for expansion, Emili Fox's two-tiered extension to a house subject to strict building regulations (see p. 226) in Australia makes use of the traditional wood verandah as a modern solution to amplifying small interior rooms. The wood decking wraps around the building to promote access to a formerly neglected back garden as well as extending most of the interior spaces to private outdoor areas and allowing natural light in through large windows and doors.

Rear Windows

The rear extension that almost completely transforms the house uses all possible access to light and outdoor space on all levels. While the front of the house maintains its period elements, the rear façade is blown open, a more transparent structure extends and brightens the interiors and the back garden becomes another desirable living space. Bedrooms become light-filled eyries, small windows are thrown open to city or landscape views while still being in the private realm at the rear of the house. The Australians seem to have a knack for adding on with panache.

Perhaps it is the preponderance of period houses similar to those in cities like London coupled with slightly less restrictive planning laws that encourages experimentation. There is also the question of available space: while urban centres are tightly packed, they are not on a par with say London or New York, so that extra patch of buildable land is more likely to exist. A number of the projects in this section are located in Australia, but something beyond sheer antipodean innovation is at work. The Victorian townhouse that Engelen Moore extended up and out (see p. 232) could be on any London or New York street. But the steel and glass structure with its spiralling, aluminium-clad stairway artfully attached to the rear of the building is altogether unique.

In a similarly grand expansion, architects Donovan Hill took a humble 1920s 'Queenslander' in Brisbane (see p. 236) and added a modular, multi-storey extension, with a roof terrace and giant door and window openings, and set it on a newly levelled site complete with an elegant seating area, large pool and translucent screen wall. Architect Stephen Varady's interventions for a house originally transformed by Australian architect Glenn Murcutt is perhaps less extravagant but no less inventive, with layers of glazing used within the house and on the exterior that bring channels of light and a constantly changing perspective (see p. 244).

On a smaller urban site in London, architect David Adjaye (see p. 242) drastically altered a factory building using glass, again pushing up and out of the original box to bring in light and burst the boundaries of limited space. This project, and others in London, like Boyarsky Murphy's great garden skylight (see p. 248), demonstrate that even in densely packed cities, where the desire for increased space and light is perhaps greatest, ingenious solutions are out there waiting to become part of the landscape.

Reconfiguring

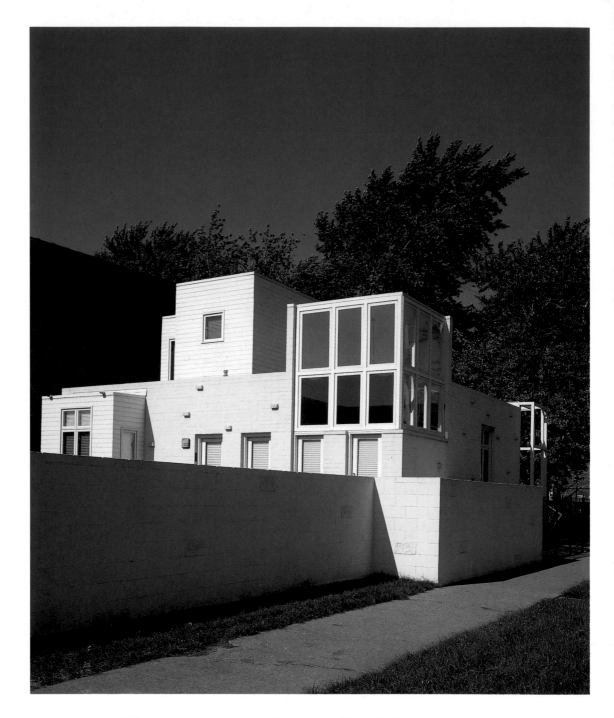

∧ **Corner house, Chicago**
'The linearity of the ordinary city street imposes a discipline on the surrounding city,' according to architects Valerio Dewalt Train, who executed an original house of 130 square metres (1400 square feet, shown above) and then returned ten years later to add another 130 square metres of space.

> Consisting mainly of the 12-metre (40 feet) aluminium cylinder, or 'tin can', the addition's aluminium skin contrasts with the masonry block but has a rectangular patterned texture that echoes the brick. Overall the rectangular shape dominates.

∧ On the original ground floor, the linear-shaped living room runs parallel to one street; the kitchen and dining spaces are set perpendicular to coincide with the other street. A rectangular box punched out from the ceiling height and lined in windows casts a vast amount of natural light but precludes any view into the house from the street.

∧ Accessed by a main spiral stairway, the aluminium-clad addition gives two more levels of living space.

> The east side of the house faces toward downtown so the architects chose to cleave the cylindrical shape in response, providing numerous and large window openings to exploit the view.

Green Bay Residence
Wisconsin
Douglas Garofalo

cross section

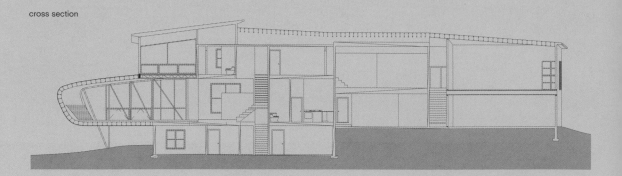

A couple with children – the father with a collection of model racing cars, the mother with an interest in horticulture and birdwatching – and an architect committed to finding non-traditional solutions to problems of structure and space came together to produce this ribbon-shaped extension to a house in an outlying area of Wisconsin. Architect Douglas Garofalo has become known for his unabashed love of nonorthagonal forms and for his pioneering use of computer animation software, such as that used by film-makers, to produce them. The couple, who were already living in this nondescript house, came upon Garofalo's work through an acquaintance and decided to take the leap from the mundane to the highly imaginative to realize their dreams for spaces dedicated to their own highly individual pursuits.

Most of the new construction and visual interest was relegated to the rear and sides of the house, leaving the front façade, which is set close to the street, with little indication of what lies beyond. Taking their cue from the husband's devotion to toy race cars, a hobby which would be accommodated separately in the new extension, the architects generated a computer model that played with the curves and straights of the racing track. This theme resulted in the curling ribbons that wind around the house to form the new series of spaces. Where one partner got to indulge his racing passion the other got a rather precarious looking birdwalk that extends out from a miniature greenhouse to a clump of trees where a number of species can be observed at leisure. In addition, and provided you do not suffer from vertigo, the perch offers an uninterrupted view over Green Bay, which lies just beyond the back garden.

In a place where weather can run to extremes and where the corroding effects of snow and ice are particularly problematic, the choice of exterior cladding tends to be vinyl siding or metal sheeting. However, the architects went for the slightly more interesting option of fibreglass, which could be moulded to the unusual shape and also allowed them to choose a distinctive colour. Corrugated metal is used elsewhere on the house, though it is painted to blend with the rest of the house's exterior. It seems there is something for everyone in this design, except perhaps the rigid conformist.

∧ The sloping back lawn is held with
a retaining wall of wooden posts that
mimics the curves of the extension and
creates a side path for the residents
to drive their tractor down to the land
beyond. The birdwalk projects from the
first-floor greenhouse to a well-populated
group of trees.

cross section

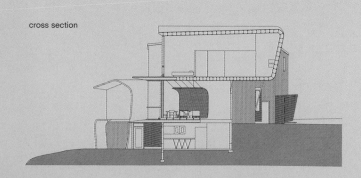

> The cantilevered living room is supported by two V-shaped steel columns that turn into steel trusses running along the inside of the wall to offer further structural support. A similar V-shaped support is used where the ribbon of spaces wraps around the building's side.

v Large and dynamic, the new living space has a wood-plank floor that runs up the wall a little way at one end but continues all the way up to become a suspended ceiling at the forefront of the room. The fireplace was designed by Douglas Garofalo and has become a popular design product.

< Corrugated-metal sheeting is a highly utilitarian material in an area that sees a great deal of snow. Painted and used in conjunction with the brightly coloured fibreglass, it takes on a more modern appearance. The projecting ribbon structure merely peeks out from the original building at this elevation.

v **Nineteenth-century barn, Maryland**
Glass insertions create rooms within an old barn while a separate system of steel plates and rods underpins the decayed structure. The dilapidated skin has been preserved while bright, modern rooms took form inside.

v A living area in the guest house and art gallery conversion by W Architecture. A service core clad in natural pine boards rises up from the lower-ground floor, formerly a hay store and now the guest quarters, to the living area here. Traditional beam supports and the A-frame ceiling retain some of the grand simplicity of the 1870s barn.

v The modern glass box with open roof
terrace protrudes from the barn that has
been preserved and supported as much
as possible. The wood cladding has only
been treated with clear varnish to protect
it from further disintegration. More glass
insertions create new spaces below and
beside the old structure.

< Rural buildings, Spring Prairie, Wisconsin

Douglas Garofalo's extensions to a collection of rural buildings add new dimension to the term 'rambling farmhouse'. The flowing form creates intimate interior spaces while enveloping and connecting the disparate elements. Windows follow both rectilinear framework and oddly shaped infill to provide maximum transparency. The extension here adds bedrooms and bathrooms for visiting family members.

∧ Set on 75 acres of land, the complex was intended as a retreat for a couple with a large extended family, offering space for large gatherings and pockets of isolation. 'The programme is analogous to a small village,' says the architect, 'where everyone knows everyone else, but where privacy is possible.' The titanium roof echoes the corrugated-metal sheets traditionally used for barn roofing.

> Though the shining curvilinear form marks a sharp break from the vernacular, its low profile and soft edges allow the original buildings to stand out and retain their own character.

v Interior spaces follow the lines of the exterior shape to create rooms with gently undulating walls and ceilings. Rooms are bathed in light from generous window openings.

>> Outdoor space was an important aspect of the design. The brief was to develop and emphasize four separate types of landscape: forest, prairie, lawn and picturesque garden.

∧ Suburban house, Southern California
Dubbed the 'black box' by the architect,
Patrick Tighe, this addition makes use of
contrasting hues and textures of wood
and filtered light.

∧ The architect refers to 'the Scandinavian
tradition of an earthy palette of natural
materials' in his approach to the structure.
The dark volume is used to highlight
the paler colours of the interior and the
surrounding landscape.

> Horizontal bands of various types of
blonde wood extend to the built-in shelves
and furniture. Metal mesh screens on the
window and door help diffuse the bright
natural light. While minimal in design, the
woods and light create a rich ambience.

> Forge, Oslo, Norway
Architects Jarmund Vigsnæs formed
a bright, modern family home by
adding large expanses of glazing
and a projecting balcony to the rear,
bringing in light and altering the
industrial box aesthetic.

>> Three brick walls were kept while
the fourth was torn down, resulting
in the glazed rear façade. The wood
cladding creates a crisp, streamlined
surface but also generates a feeling
of warmth and domestication.

⋀ The idea of the box pervaded the new design in that the architects created 'boxes of private spaces', which were then 'hung' within the volume of the 10-metre-high (33 feet) interior.

< Continuity is achieved by using wood throughout the interior, and transparency is enhanced through the open stair rails and glass-topped partitions.

⋀ An open-work staircase rising through the full height of the interior volume and lit by a skylight emphasizes the loftlike interior, while intersecting with the room boxes.

Cremorne House
Near Sydney, Australia
Emili Fox

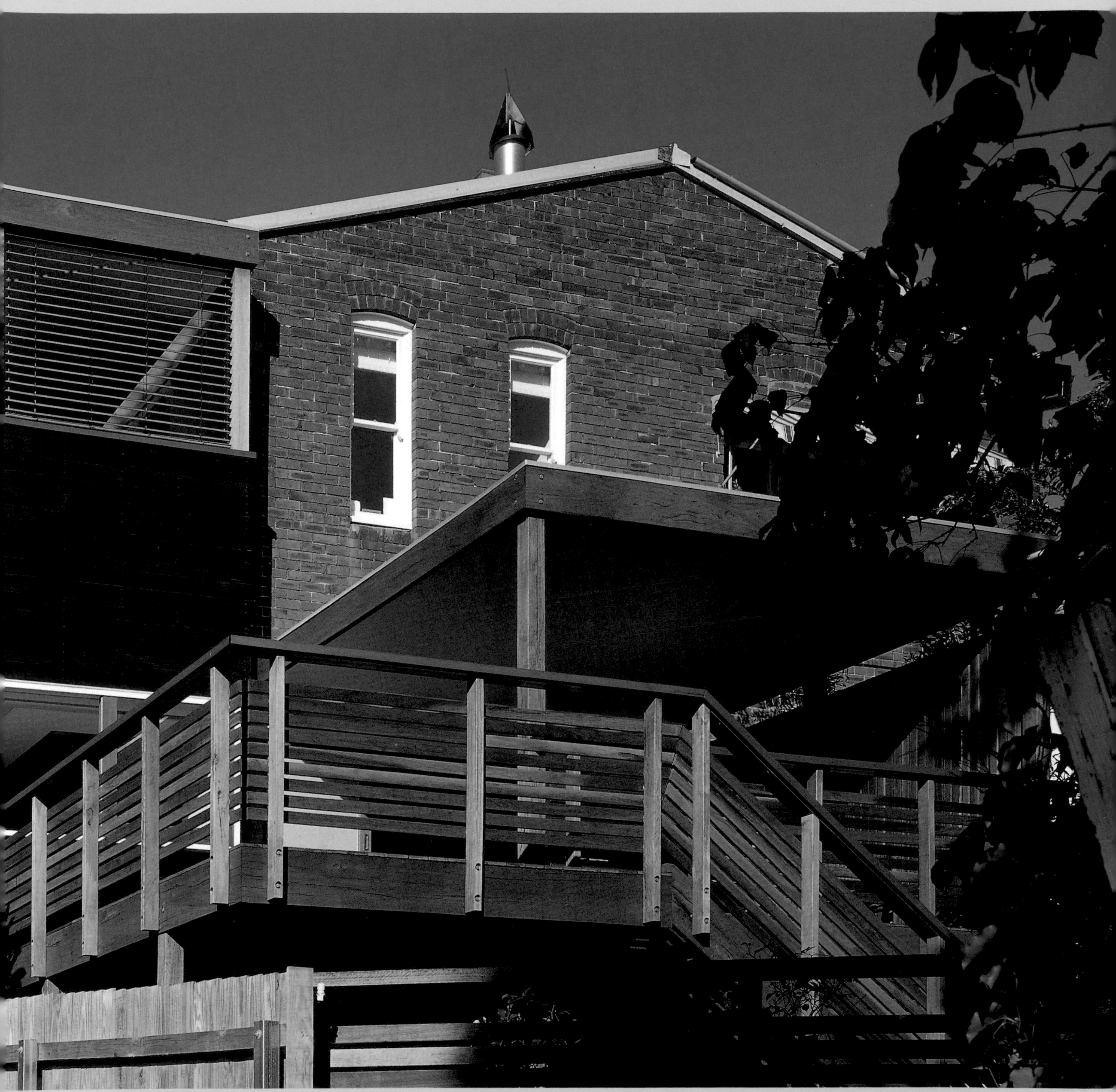

∧ Western red-cedar cladding, charcoal-stained in places, helps a new two-storey structure harmonize in tone and colour with the original Edwardian brick building. But, the sharp geometry, cut-out window spaces and contrasting hues have a decidedly modern appeal.

< The new living room extends its reach beyond the end wall and onto the new deck. When fully opened, it becomes a seamless passage between indoors and out. Enclosed outdoor spaces and an open verandah are infinitely useful for a family with small children.

< The open-plan kitchen and dining area has a clean, modern feeling. The recycled spotted gum flooring flows out onto the deck areas.

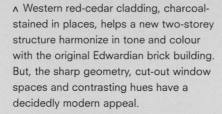

side elevation

Contrasting colours and textures of wood can be used to great effect, as in this extension by Emili Fox near Sydney, Australia, which marries period and contemporary ideas of living space. A family of five were already living in the 1908 semi-detached house, which had been built as part of a complex of ten residences in a design that had given little consideration to views or light. The house had already undergone partitioning into two separate flats and then reconversion to a single-family dwelling. In the process, the small rooms, approached by a narrow hallway, had not been enhanced, the outdoor area had been ignored and the whole house had fallen into a state of disrepair.

Asked to give logic to and amplify the space, but within strict planning laws and a limited budget, Fox added a two-storey, timber-framed structure that feeds into one side of the existing house on the ground and first floor. The house now has full northern exposure. The living room, though not a vast space, expands onto the new deck. On the floor above, the children's bedrooms also open onto a new, enclosed deck, creating an ideal play area for them. The timber structure winds around to the back of the house to form another deck area that gives ready access to the previously disused back garden and private tennis court.

While many of the period features were retained and reconditioned, the new structure, sympathetic in terms of materials and overall proportion, offers a more open and modern feeling to the interior and exterior. Inside the rooms have been opened up to take advantage of the new terraces and the light they allow, while large, movable louvred panels and sliding doors provide a seamless transition to the outdoor areas and create more intimate, enclosed spaces. The house has become more spacious and more flexible without the need for an overtly grand gesture or price tag.

< Sliding window panels make the living space almost fully openable when used in conjunction with the sliding doors leading onto the deck area. The louvred design means that the space is never totally devoid of natural light and defeats the need for window coverings, keeping the interior streamlined.

∧ The open kitchen/dining/living space was created by knocking together the small, awkward rooms. The linear design, aided by the built-in seating, window frames and floor pattern, directs focus toward the new outdoor deck.

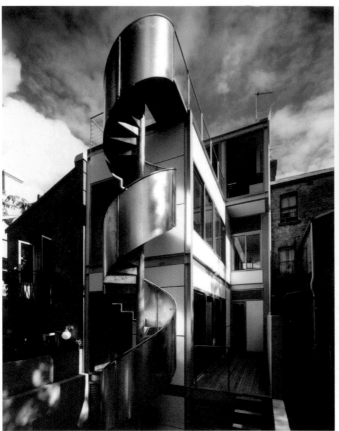

∧ Victorian townhouse, Sydney

The owner of this house wanted to divide the property into a home upstairs and a flat to let on the ground floor and basement. Architects Engelen Moore demolished the dilapidated rear section of the house and rebuilt it with an exposed steel-framed structure, a new courtyard and a spiral staircase. A roof terrace was also added.

∧ Highlighting the shortcomings of the Victorian terrace, the architects explain that in the existing house 'all the major rooms address the street and the ancillary functions are relegated to the rear wing with a single small window to take advantage of the view'. In addition to extending the rear, they created open-plan living spaces to amplify further the interiors. The open attic floor overlooks the living room and serves as a display area for the owner's artworks.

< As the house is used to store and exhibit the owner's collection of Asian artifacts and modern art, an interior of large, blank planes was suitable. Details, such as timber flooring and spots of colour, add character to the otherwise spare environment.

∧ Rooms were re-oriented to the rear
of the house, rather than the street side,
toward the view and the new courtyard.
The first floor is a bright eyrie, illuminated
with large glass doors and skylights,
which extends to a wood-decked terrace.

< The spiral staircase accesses the rear
garden and garage from the roof without
disturbing tenants on the lower level.
The levelled courtyard is a usable outdoor
space on a site that falls 10 metres
(33 feet) from front to back.

∧ In the confines of a narrow passage,
an open flight of stairs makes the area
feel less cramped and allows plenty of
light to reach the corridor.

∧ **Detached family home,
near Brisbane, Australia**
A 1920s 'Queenslander', a house with
timber cladding and Edwardian details,
is typical of the houses in this suburb
outside Brisbane. The residents wanted
to refurbish the interior but also to
add space and asked Donovan Hill
to help them.

∨ The Great Opening is a key feature
of the extended house, allowing the
various staggered rooms to share the
view and emphasizing the flow between
the house and the reclaimed outdoor
space, which has been designed to
coincide in form and proportion to the
extension. The carport at left and the
sitting area at right act as screens
to provide privacy. The carport, with
its translucent panels, appears like
a great lantern.

∧ Due to its steep incline and small
amount of level space, the back garden
was previously unused. The architects
used the spoil from digging the pool to
create the spacious back garden 'room',
which is flanked by a carport on one
side and a sitting area on the other.

> Apart from needed renovation,
the plan was to leave the existing building
as it was and to add space through the
development of a 'miniature city', with
a private residents' suite and such public
spaces as a kitchen, terraces and guest
bedrooms arrayed on numerous split
levels or folding floor planes. Here, a
dining area off the kitchen is only partly
enclosed before the 'Great Opening'
overlooking the garden.

∨ One of several transitional areas, this
space has an open balcony overlooking
the garden. Wood adds warmth to the
clean interior. The floating staircase and
partition wall carry the theme of continuity
through the spaces.

> A sliding metal screen closes the Great Opening at the back. Separate glazed sections also allow different areas to be enclosed.

>> Exploiting all the available volume possible under the building codes, the architects were also careful to make use of every possible view and to manipulate views according to principles espoused by Adolf Loos.

v A seeming fun house of shifting planes is actually a carefully constructed geometry that allows maximum openness but also privacy and seclusion. Wood adds a luxurious quality to a project executed on a fairly modest budget.

∧ Set in a cantilevered structure, the second-floor bedroom has a fully glazed end wall and a view of the old parish church.

< As it was not possible to receive planning permission to create new foundations at the rear of the building, the architect extended the space horizontally through the cantilevered structure. The roof of the projecting volume is used as a glass-enclosed terrace and is accessed from the glass-walled roof extension.

∧ **Manufacturing building, London**
Architect David Adjaye inserted a steel-and-glass structure inside the shell of a building. The new structure projects beyond the roofline to offer views over the city, and interiors throughout benefit from added light sources.

<< Bungalow, near Sydney

In 1969, architect Glenn Murcutt created an addition to the rear ground floor of this bungalow, removing walls and drawing attention to the garden outside. The new owners asked Stephen Varady to 'revitalize' the ground floor, redesigning the bedroom, bathroom and kitchen and adding a new private 'retreat' for parents. This new first-floor extension includes a study, bedroom, bathroom, dressing area and courtyard. A 'Barcelona Pavilion–inspired carport' (not shown) was also designed.

< The new master bedroom, with its 3-x-3.6-metre (10 x 12 feet) steel-framed sliding-glass door and frameless glass balustrade, was designed to give 'the illusion of sleeping in the canopy of the trees'.

> Glass is the main material in this extension, chosen by the architect for its 'transparent, translucent and solid' properties. Seamless glass panels frame the enclosure, shower and bath. The glazed roof washes the whole room in light and the fact that the room is only 1.5-metres (5 feet) wide becomes irrelevant with the lack of opaque partitions.

v In the new first-floor hallway and dressing area, doors and wall panels stop short of ceiling height to allow light from the glazed section at right to penetrate other rooms. Varady's aim for transparency follows the theme established in the initial alterations made by Glenn Murcutt.

v The mirror from the bathing area shows the glazed interior courtyard, which leads to the master bedroom. The courtyard has a glass floor that filters light through to the space below. Here the 'layers of glass' used to amplify and extend the relatively small spaces can be seen in full effect.

∧ 1950s house, London

'Our brief was to add a third floor and to make the rather gloomy house lighter throughout, to rethink the staircase and entry and, as the project developed, to build a new extension to the garden,' say architects Boyarsky Murphy of their design for a London residence built in the particularly austere manner of post-World War II British housing.

< Glass plays a primary role in the interventions. While the brick addition on the top floor adheres to the style of the existing and neighbouring buildings, it also has a continuous glazed clerestory window on three sides and oversized sliding glass doors at the rear.

∧ The new garden room with three glass walls and giant skylight brings attention to the garden while also drawing much-needed light into the interior spaces.

Methods and Materials

After the initial decision to expand has been taken and ideas considered of where the space will go, it is time to focus on style, size, effect. Do you want wide open spaces or cosy retreats? Are you thinking outdoor spaces or internal arrangements? Do you want something similar to what you have, only bigger? Or are you someone who wants to make a statement, a clear departure from old to new?

Following are a collection of details that highlight certain aspects of some of the additions presented earlier. The focus is on the material or particular theme that makes the extension unusual or helps to define its unique character. Materials carry certain connotations: glass and concrete are seen as cool and modern; wood is often considered less formal and more homely. As you look through these examples you will see that building clichés do not always hold and the feeling you get from a building depends on the mix of materials, the form they have been given or the setting (or existing structure) in which they have been used.

There is also the opportunity to look at a range of building details – windows, skylights, stairways – which architects will obviously have a view on in the overall scheme of their design, but which present a variety of options that the average homeowner may not have considered. Choices for all these elements can be overwhelming, but looking at them individually may help you decide what best fits your vision for your home or may help you to choose something completely new and adventurous.

Wood

Most people are familiar with the warm, welcoming qualities of wood: the glow of a polished oak floor or the satisfying weathered patina of cedar cladding. Many wood products are environmentally friendly, being harvested from sustainable forests, and so have added green attraction. But, wood can also be used to create a sharp, modern-looking structure. Plywood, instead of finely finished planks, can be cheap to use but can convey a contemporary edge. Continuous wood-clad surfaces that eschew fanciful details have a sleek, minimal quality that still carries the warmth inherent in the material. No matter how it is used, wood will always have a certain appeal, but that appeal can be exploited in different ways.

v Clockwise from below: Neugebauer + Rösch, p. 142; Patrick Tighe, p. 220; Atelier Bow-Wow, p. 198; Archifactory, p. 147; and8, p. 162.

Glass

As Australian architect Stephen Varady points out 'the perception of all spaces is increased through the use of glass'. If one of the aims of an extension is to bring in light then residents and their architects will invariably be faced with both the costs and the glittering possibilities of glass. Using glass in large expanses connotes a degree of glamour and luxury, but used creatively and in key positions it can be affordable. If the appeal of transparency and light are just too great to impose restrictions, glass exists that will meet structural and thermal standards, allowing you to build almost anything. As shown, glass can sit elegantly next to stone or brick, in the urban or rural environment and always creates an enchanting, glowing presence.

v Clockwise from below: Stephen Varady, p. 246; Wilkinson King, p. 91; Deborah Saunt and David Hills, p.166; Paul Archer, p.156; Paul Archer, p. 56.

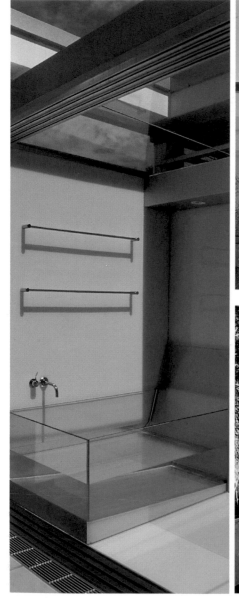

Concrete, a favourite building material of the late-twentieth century, has a reputation for being hard, thick and unforgiving. However, its versatility has brought architects to rely on it as a building material. Formed into varying shapes and offering reliable structural support, it can be left rough and naturally grey, pigment-dyed or polished to a high sheen. The concrete structure lined with seamless glass walls has become an icon of modern design, presenting a seductive image of clean-line living with an exciting tension between the impervious solidity of one material and the transparent fragility of the other. While it may seem like a material reserved for foundations and retaining walls, concrete happily comes into its own as a featured building material.

v Clockwise from below: Rudy Ricciotti, p. 107; Drewes + Strenge, p. 155; Daly Genik, p. 185; Studio For Architecture, p. 98.

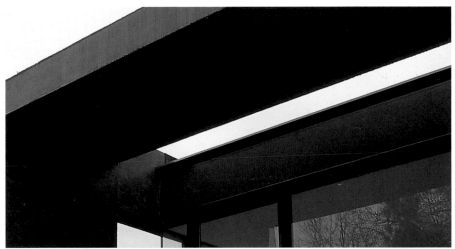

Skin

Whatever the internal structure of a building, it is the exterior skin that conveys the most immediate feeling of a style, period or theme. The most familiar building skins are wood, brick, stone or a render laid over the top of these elements. Today, however, clients and architects are experimenting with a diverse range of cladding, from metals like aluminium and corrugated sheeting to bright panels of titanium like those that wrap the Guggenheim in Bilbao. Plastics, too, such as polycarbonate panels and formed polyurethane, are now manufactured to maintain thermal values and are legitimate exterior barriers. Often it is a combination of familiar and traditional materials with something more adventurous that bestows a unique character on a building.

v Clockwise from below: Douglas Garofalo, p. 217; Jakob + MacFarlane, p. 32; Marmol Radziner, p. 92; Lorcan O'Herlihy, p. 25; One Architecture, p. 82; Valerio Dewalt Train, p. 209; Simon Conder, p. 43; Manuel Herz, p. 31.

Skylights and Floorlights

Skylights in domestic spaces have come a long way from the leaky, dirt-attracting images of yore, and in densely packed urban spaces they offer an extremely practical solution to opening up small, dark rooms. However, the real attraction of skylights (and the corresponding floorlights) is the innovative ways in which they can be used. Whether it is positioning a small patch of structural glass to allow natural light to flow through more than one floor in a house, or punching through a previously solid roof, or simply adding unusually shaped windows in unimagined spaces, the possibilities for creating unexpected channels of light can change the way we think about interior spaces and how we live in them.

v Clockwise from below: David Adjaye,
p. 190; Springett Mackay, p. 174; GAD
Architecture, p. 192; Engelen Moore,
p. 235; Jakob + MacFarlane, p. 33;
Manuel Herz, p. 31; M³ Architects,
p. 101; Boyarsky Murphy, p. 251.

Windows

Though the practical function of a window is to let in light and let people see out, the style and position of windows say a lot about a house. While most of us live in buildings with regular window openings determined by the style the house was built in, an extension allows us to re-think this restriction. It may be that privacy is essential and window openings must create as little exposure as possible, or it may be that you find having your house's visual barriers thrown open liberating. Also, there is the challenge of introducing large glazed areas that prevent views inward while letting in maximum amounts of light. If the cost of large, thermally efficient glazed panels is an issue, standardized windows can be varied in number and position to form a unique identity.

v Clockwise from below: Valerio Dewalt
Train, p. 207; Kennedy & Violich, p. 67;
One Architecture, p. 84; Sam Marshall,
p. 28; Architecture-Studio, p. 27;
Manuel Herz, p. 30; Sanya Polescuk,
p. 77; Stephen Varady, p. 149.

Indoor Outdoor

More than a question of climate, this is a philosophy about inhabiting not only the space within but also that without. Some people are happy secluded within the confines of a cosy, well-heated house, while others enjoy the great sense of expansion that comes with having immediate outdoor access or an almost imperceptible barrier between the inside and out. Glass walls and doors are the most common ways to achieve this seamless blend, but it is also to do with larger than average doors and windows, with spaces at the same level, with using a continuous stretch of material on the floor or walls that reaches from the interior to the exterior and with having as few visual obstructions as possible between your interior space and its reach to the natural surroundings.

∨ Clockwise from below: m³architecture, p. 176; Vincent Van Duysen, p. 118; Simon Conder, p. 52; Marmol Radziner, p. 116; David Adjaye, p. 59; Lorcan O'Herlihy, p. 21; Jarmund Vigsnæs, p. 134.

Landscaping

Whether or not an extension feeds into the garden, the construction often involves digging up around the house and so arises the possibility of putting it all back in a more desirable and accessible way. Garden extensions benefit from coordinated landscaping that enhances views and facilitates the blend between indoors and out. Planting and paving schemes that lead to or away from the house draw attention to the outdoors and achieve a sense of integration. Particularly with ground-floor extensions, it is wise to consider the surrounding vegetation, whether it will be semi-wild native planting or contemporary hardscape with outdoor furnishings and designer pots for a more ordered experience with nature and a focus on places to relax and entertain.

∨ Clockwise from below: Marmol Radziner, p. 95; Douglas Garofalo, p. 211; Douglas Garofalo, p. 219; Daly Genik, p. 180; Daly Genik, p. 50; Marmol Radziner, p. 114; Rudy Ricciotti, p. 108; Simon Conder, p. 55.

Stairs

Necessary elements that architects often struggle with, stairs take up large amounts of precious space but can be a feature in themselves. While it is possible to purchase stairs practically off the shelf, it would be a shame not to consider the alternatives that make a stairway much more than a means of access. Light is a major consideration: will the structure be a boxed-in passage all on its own; will the sides and treads be left open to allow the free flow of light; will a crowning skylight brighten the vertical corridor? Some architects relish the challenge of stairs, of creating something beautifully sculptural, while other designers exploit the utilitarian possibilities of hiding services in stair walls or of building display shelves, lighting features or handy half-level spaces.

v Clockwise from below: Engelen Moore, p. 232; Patrick Tighe, p. 188; Jarmund Vigsnæs, p. 225; Neugebauer + Rösch, p. 145; Drewes + Strenge, p. 150; Donovan Hill, p. 239.

Contact Details

Adjaye/Associates
David Adjaye
23–28 Penn Street
London N1 5DL
UK

T +44 (0)20 7739 4969
F + 44 (0)20 7739 3484
E info@adjaye.com
W www.adjaye.com

and8 ARCHITEKTEN
Achim Aisslinger, Andreas Bracht
Margaretenstrasse 15
20357 Hamburg
Germany

T +49 (0)40 430 8811
F +49 (0)40 430 8887
E office@and8.de
W www.and8.de

Paul Archer Design
Paul Archer
3D2 Zetland House
5–25 Scrutton Street
London EC2A 4HJ
UK

T +44 (0)20 7729 2729
F +44 (0)20 7739 8476
E lisaharrison@paularcherdesign.co.uk
W www.paularcherdesign.co.uk

ARCHIFACTORY.DE
Matthias Herrmann und Matthias Koch
Am Hunnepoth 6
D-44869 Bochum
Germany

T +49 (0)232 799 4762
F +49 (0)232 799 4764
E office@archifactory.de
W www.archifactory.de

Architect Marshall
Sam Marshall
PO Box 780
Darlinghurst NSW 1300
Australia

T +61 (0)2 9310 7555
F +61 (0)2 9310 4144
E sammarshall@ozemail.com.au

Architecture-Studio
10, rue Lacuée

75012 Paris
France

T +33 (0)1 43 45 18 00
F +33 (0)1 43 43 81 43
E as@architecture-studio.fr
W www.architecture-studio.fr

Artifact Design + Construction
Christopher Kilbridge, Salvatore Tranchina
121 West 27th Street, Suite 705
New York, NY 10001
USA

T +1 212 206 7945
E mail@artifactonline.com
W www.artifactonline.com

Atelier Bow-Wow
Yoshiharu Tsukamoto, Momoyo Kaijima
1-24-3 Higashi Shibuya
Tokyo 150-0011
Japan

T +81 (0)3 5774 6508
F +81 (0)3 5468 6028
E info@bow-wow.jp
W www.bow-wow.jp

Bayer Uhrig Architekten
Beethovenstrasse 54–56
67655 Kaiserslautern
Germany

T +49 (0)631 212 25
F +49 (0)631 310 5883
E architekten@bayer-uhrig.de
W www.bayer-uhrig.com

Boyarsky Murphy Architects
Nicholas Boyarsky, Nicola Murphy
64 Oakley Square
London NW1 1NJ
UK

T +44 (0)20 7388 3572
F +44 (0)20 7691 0847
E n2@boyarskymurphy.com
W www.boyarskymurphy.com

Jim Burton
BLIP Design
3235 42nd Avenue West
Seattle, WA 98199
USA

T +1 206 501 8746
F +1 206 284 6479

E burtonj530@aol.com
W www.blipdesign.com

Simon Conder Associates
Simon Conder
Nile Street Studios
8 Nile Street
London N1 7RF
UK

T +44 (0)20 7251 2144
F +44 (0)20 7251 2145
E sca@simonconder.co.uk
W www.simonconder.co.uk

Daly Genik
Kevin Daly, Chris Genik
1558 Tenth Street-C
Santa Monica, CA 90401
USA

T +1 310 656 3180
F +1 310 656 3183
E info@dalygenik.com
W www.dalygenik.com

Deborah Saunt David Hills Architects
Deborah Saunt, David Hills
8 Iliffe Yard
London SE17 3QA
UK

T +44 (0)20 7703 3555
F +44 (0)20 7703 3890
E info@dsdha.co.uk
W www.dsdha.co.uk

Donovan Hill
112 Bowen Street
Spring Hill QLD 4000
Brisbane
Australia

T +61 (0)7 3831 3255
F +61 (0)7 3831 3266
E mail@donovanhill.com.au
W www.donovanhill.com.au

Drewes + Strenge Architekten
Bahnhofstrasse 10a
33442 Herzebrock-Clarholz
Germany

T +49 (0)524 53 208
F +49 (0)524 518 710
E info@drewesstrenge.com
W www.drewesstrenge.com

ENGELENMOORE
Tina Engelen, Ian Moore
44 McLachlan Avenue
Rushcutters Bay NSW 2011
Sydney
Australia

T +61 (0)2 9380 4099
F +61 (0)2 9380 4302
F architects@engelenmoore.com.au
W www.engelenmoore.com.au

Fox Johnston
Emili Fox
105 Reservoir Street
Surry Hills NSW 2010
Sydney
Australia

T +61 (0)2 9211 2700
F +61 (0)2 9211 2785
E emili@foxjohnston.com.au
W www.foxjohnston.com.au

GAD Architecture and Design
Gokhan Avcioglu, Ozlem Ercil
9 Desbrosses Street 515
New York NY 10013
USA

T +1 917 679 4971
T +1 646 258 1777
F +1 212 941 6496
E gadny@gadarchitecture.com
W www.gadarchitecture.com

Hans Gangoly
Volksgartenstrasse 18
A-8020 Graz
Austria

T +43 (0)316 717 550
F +43 (0)316 717 5506
E office@gangoly.at
W www.gangoly.at

Garofalo Architects
Douglas Garofalo
3752 North Ashland Avenue
Chicago, IL 60613
USA

T +1 773 975 2069
F +1 773 975 3005
E doug@garofaloarchitects.com
W www.garofaloarchitects.com

Manuel Herz
Zugweg 16
D-50677 Cologne
Germany

T +49 (0)221 932 9293
F +49 (0)221 932 9295
E office@manuelherz.com
W www.manuelherz.com

Jakob + MacFarlane
13, rue des petites écuries
75010 Paris
France

T +33 (0)1 44 79 05 72
F +33 (0)1 48 00 97 93
E jakmak@club-internet.fr
W www.jakobmacfarlane.com

Jarmund Vigsnæs (JVA)
Einar Jarmund, Håkon Vigsnæs,
Alessandra Kosberg
Arkitekter MNAL
Hausmannsgate 6
0186 Oslo
Norway

T +47 22 99 43 43
F +47 22 99 43 53
E jva@jva.no
W www.jva.no

KENNEDY & VIOLICH ARCHITECTURE, LTD.
160 North Washington Street, 8th Floor
Boston, MA 02114
USA

T +1 617 367 3784
F +1 617 367 3727
E info@kvarch.net
W www.kvarch.net

Korteknie Stuhlmacher Architecten
Rien Korteknie, Mechthild Stuhlmacher
Postbus 25012
3001 HA Rotterdam
the Netherlands

T +31 (0) 10 425 94 41
F +31 (0) 10 466 51 55
E mail@kortekniestuhlmacher.nl
W www.kortekniestuhlmacher.nl

LABICS
via dei Magazzini Generali 16
00154 Rome
Italy

T +39 06 57 28 80 49
F +39 06 57 13 78 08
E info@labics.it
W www.labics.it

M³ Architects
Ken Hutt, Nadi Jahangiri
49 Kingsway Place
Sans Walk
London EC1R 0LU
UK

T +44 (0)20 7253 7255
F +44 (0)20 7253 7266
E post@m3architects.com
W www.m3architects.com

m³architecture
24 Gore Street
Albion Q 4010
Australia

T +61 (0)7 3262 5711
F +61 (0)7 3262 5722
E info@m3architecture.com
W www.m3architecture.com

Marmol Radziner + Associates
12210 Nebraska Avenue
Los Angeles, CA 90025
USA

T +1 310 826 6222
F +1 310 826 6226
E info@marmol-radziner.com
W www.marmol-radziner.com

Neugebauer + Rösch
Sonja Neugebauer, Robert Rösch
Eberhardstrasse 61
70173 Stuttgart
Germany

T +49 (0)711 2484 7780
F +49 (0)711 2484 77822
E info@neugebauer-roesch.de
W www.neugebauer-roesch.de

Lorcan O'Herlihy Architects
5709 Mesmer Avenue
Culver City, CA 90230
USA

T +1 310 398 0394
F +1 310 398 2675
E loh@loharchitects.com
W www.loharchitects.com

oceanD | Boston | New York | London
Panther House
East Block, Second Floor, Unit 1
38 Mount Pleasant
London WC1 X0AP
UK

T +44 (0)20 7833 0744
E tverebes@oceanD.com
W www.oceanD.com

office of richard davignon Architecture, ordA
Richard Davignon
136, b1 2451 Dieppe Avenue SW
Calgary
Alberta T3E 7K1
Canada

T +1 403 282 6082
F +1 403 282 7941
E richard@orda.ca
W www.orda.ca

One Architecture
Matthijs Bouw
Vliegtuigstraat 26
1059 CL Amsterdam
the Netherlands

T +31 (0)20 470 00 40
F +31 (0)20 676 40 19
E office@onearchitecture.nl
W www.onearchitecture.nl

Sanya Polescuk Architects
Sanya Polescuk
8a Baynes Mews
London NW3 5BH
UK

T +44 (0)20 7431 8580
F +44 (0)20 7435 8341
E enquiries@polescukarchitects.com
W www.polescukarchitects.com

Rudy Ricciotti Architecte
17 boulevard Victor Hugo
83150 Bandol
France

T +33 (0)4 94 29 52 61
F +33 (0)4 94 32 45 25
E rudy.ricciotti@wanadoo.fr

Springett Mackay Architecture
70 Hatton Garden, First Floor
London EC1N 8JT
UK

T +44 (0)20 7692 5950
F +44 (0)20 7692 5951
E mail@sm-arch.com
W www.sm-arch.com

Studio For Architecture
Mehrdad Hadighi
312 Bryant Street
Buffalo, NY 14222
USA

T/F +1 716 886 7218
E studioforarchitecture@yahoo.com

Henning Stummel Architects Ltd
Henning Stummel
6 Shouldham Street
London W1H 5FG
UK

T +44 (0)20 7724 2639
F +44 (0)20 7724 3931
E mail@henningstummelarchitects.co.uk
W henningstummelarchitects.co.uk

Tighe Architecture
Patrick J Tighe
1632 Ocean Park Boulevard
Santa Monica, CA 90405
USA

T +1 310 450 8823
F +1 310 450 8273
E info@tighearchitecture.com
W www.tighearchitecture.com

Valerio Dewalt Train Associates
500 North Dearborn, Suite 900
Chicago, IL 60610
USA

T +1 312 332 0363
F +1 312 332 4727
E info@buildordie.com
W www.buildordie.com

Vincent Van Duysen Architects
Vincent Van Duysen
Lombardenvest 34
B-2000 Antwerp
Belgium

T +32 (0)3 205 91 90
F +32 (0)3 204 01 38
E vincent@vincentvanduysen.com
W www.vincentvanduysen.com

Stephen Varady Architecture
PO Box 105
St. Peters NSW 2044
Sydney
Australia

T +61 (0)2 9516 4044
F +61 (0)2 9516 4541
E svarady@bigpond.com
W www.stephenvarady.com

W Architecture
Barbara Wilks, Alexandros E Washburn
127 West 25th Street, 12th Floor
New York, NY 10001
USA

T +1 212 981 3933
F +1 212 981 3979
W www.w-architecture.com

Wilkinson King Architects
Julian King, Chantal Wilkinson
Unit 6 Burghley Yard
106 Burghley Road
London NW5 1AL
UK

T +44 (0)20 7284 1975
F +44 (0)20 7284 1984
E architects@wilkinsonking.com
W www.wilkinsonking.com

Photography Credits

Index

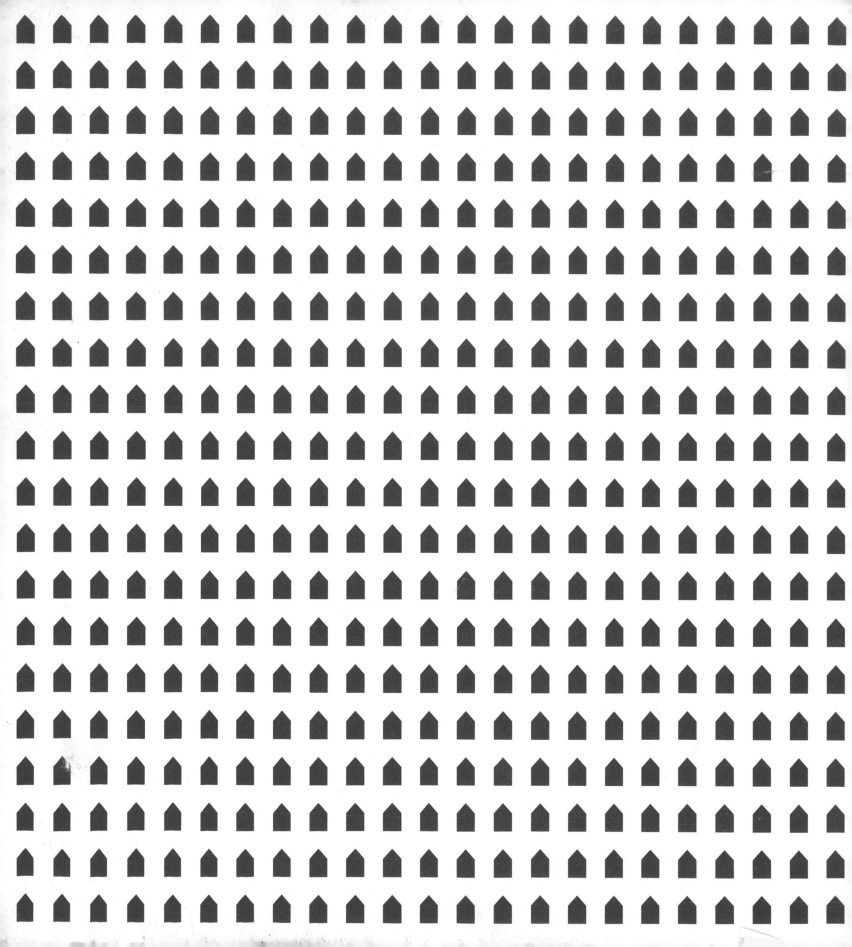